My Daddy Hurt Me

My Daddy Hurt Me

By

Isabelle A. Fiola

iafiola@ymail.com

Acknowledgements

It's been a long time awaiting the completion of this project. This book took a decade in years and many re-writes in work. I would like to thank the following people for walking with me during my healing journey and the writing of this book.

To my Divine Creator who was there every step of the way with guidance and direction.

To my daughters who grew with me during my healing journey. Their patience and forgiveness along the way is my most treasured reward.

To my closest friend Jacqueline L., who kept close contact with me and freely allowed me share my tears and angers without judgment.

To my niece, Michelle and her mother for their loving encouragement. I can always count on their smiles to uplift my day.

To the people in my life whom I have crossed paths with, I am thankful for their presence throughout my journey. May they find peace, not as the world gives peace, but as Christ gives His peace.

Table of Contents

Part 1

Memories Play Back

In a small Canadian prairie town named Laurance, a funeral for a community member named Darren Havonick was to be held. The deceased was divorced and left to mourn his twenty-one year old daughter, Cathy, and his son Jake, who was fourteen. Also left to mourn were his mother, six siblings, friends and relatives; his father predeceased him. Cathy managed the arrangements of the funeral and invited her Aunt Malinda and Uncle Hubert, on her mother's side, to sing *Amazing Grace*. Hubert was a husky fifty-one year old man. Malinda was five foot five, slim, forty-five years of age and twice divorced. She had two adult daughters from her first marriage, Nadine and Suzanne.

Malinda was undergoing professional help in order to build up her confidence after the many losses in her life. Her counsellor explained that self-esteem was part of the groundwork for her recovery. She wanted to look her best at the funeral so she thought to call her former hair stylist, Leo, whose talent was modern and sought after. She decided that she could not afford such a luxury. Malinda had discontinued going to him after her most recent divorce because she had to lower her lifestyle.

Her counsellor suggested the use of a catchphrase when she feared taking a step: *feel the fear and do it anyway*. With that slogan in mind, she changed her mind and phoned Leo. When he answered the phone, Malinda apologized for calling on such short notice and said, "I've been asked to sing at my brother-in-law's funeral the day after tomorrow and I need something done with my hair, even if it's just a quick haircut." Without waiting for his answer, she added, "I can even do the shampoo and blow-dry my own hair at home."

Happily, Leo said, "I can see you first thing in the morning before I start my appointments. Can you come in at eight?"

"Yes!" Malinda answered.

Leo replied, "Good, I'll see you then."

When Malinda arrived for the appointment, the curly black haired young Leo greeted her with his charming smile and said, "Hello Malinda, it's good to see you! Come on in." Leo had emigrated from Italy and proudly owned and operated his own studio in the city. He remembered how Malinda liked coffee and poured her a cup. He escorted her to his styling chair.

"How's life been treating you?" asked Leo.

"Well, I got divorced and moved to the city. I live in a condo with a nice man named Richard. I'm now a new grandmother," she answered.

Leo commented, "I'm sorry to hear about the divorce, but congratulations on your first grandchild. You're too young to be a grandmother."

Malinda answered, "I was there in the delivery room you know. I was the first one to touch him other than the doctor and staff. I never thought being a grandmother would be so wonderful."

Leo assessed the condition of her hair and recommended that she try a new hair colour. He opened the doors of his supply cabinet and took out some colour samples to show her. Malinda said, "They are very nice but I just want you to give me a quick haircut.

Leo persisted, "Look at this colour. I think it would look nice on you." Malinda thought it would not hurt to just look. A colouring would cost more than what she anticipated to spend. Leo pulled out a hair sample from the colour case and put it against her temple. "It's sort of red!" said Malinda.

Leo responded, "It's not red, it's copper."

"I never had red hair, Leo," she protested.

Then Leo said, "The colour of your roots shows you were once a dark blond but with age, the color turned auburn."

"That's right; I was blond up until my mid thirties. The sun used to give me really nice streaks of blond hair in the summertime," said Malinda.

Malinda looked in the large mirror facing her as Leo held the sample against her hair. Then he said, "This colour looks especially good on ladies with blue eyes such as yours." Fearing such a drastic change, Malinda began to feel uptight. Leo reassured her and said, "This colour would only brighten your hair but not so much that it would be drastic. It would give you a nice boost. It's up to you."

Malinda knew Leo well enough to trust him. She took a deep breath and said, "Okay, Leo, do it."

After the colour treatment, Leo cut and styled Malinda's hair. As he blow dried her hair the new colour began to emerge. When he was finished styling her hair, Leo stood proudly behind the styling chair and looked at Malinda in the mirror. Malinda said, "I like it."

Leo said, "Oh, it looks great!"

"You did a good job, Leo. Thank you.

"You're welcome," Leo proudly answered.

The next day, Malinda and Hubert met early at the funeral in order to practice singing together one last time before mass began. Hubert was with his wife and Malinda was with Richard. When they entered the church, Cathy was there to greet them. She was breathing rapidly. "Hi, Auntie Maddy. I'm so-o-o glad you're here. Thanks so much for agreeing to sing." She heaved a huge sigh of relief.

Malinda hugged her and replied, "I wouldn't think of turning you down." Cathy turned to Hubert and gave him a hug, then accompanied the two to the front where the choir section was.

"Could you sing at the end and just before the priest blesses my dad in the coffin and just before the pallbearers take him away?"

Malinda answered, "Of course." Then she added, "You've done a great job with the funeral arrangements."

Cathy countered, "Not really. There are so many problems. First, Uncle Ted got sick and can't make it. I had to find another pallbearer - this morning! Then the caterers made lunch for one hundred and forty people instead of two hundred and forty. I had to run to the grocery store and buy more cold cuts and bread. You *are* staying for lunch?"

Malinda said, "Of course! And don't worry. Everything will be just fine. You've worked hard at giving your dad a great funeral. You are such a good daughter."

Her eye on the front doorway, Cathy said, "I have to go. I'll see you guys later."

Hubert's wife and Richard sat nearby. Hubert reached in his suit pocket and took out a wrinkled piece of paper and read his handwritten notes. Then he took out a folded song sheet. He glanced at the large black clock on the wall and said, "Aren't you nervous, Malinda?" Malinda was about to answer when Hubert added, "Just look at all these people coming in?" This time he waited for her answer.

"Am I nervous?" she repeated.

Hubert asked another question, "What if I make a mistake and the song gets ruined!"

Malinda answered, "Don't think about the people. Sing to God who gave you a wonderful voice and let Him touch the people with your song."

Hubert retorted, "But it's still my voice!"

Malinda said, "Just sing to God and you'll be alright." They quietly practiced the music, then sat down and waited.

Malinda knew the Havonicks for many years. She first met Darren in the sixties through his brother, JJ; they were teenagers. Darren's father was alive then, but he was wheelchair bound, stricken with Multiple Sclerosis. She remembers how his sons would light his cigarettes and pour him a drink. His daughters spoon-fed him. A nurse came by once a week to monitor his vitals. The family was poor. Their house showed signs of neglect and had no indoor plumbing. They kept a cow, a pig and some free range chickens for milk, meat and eggs. The yard was cluttered with car parts and broken down old rusty farm equipment. Next to the house was a garage with a warped roof. The Havonick boys all shared the same passion for cars. JJ had older brothers who taught him auto mechanics and, in turn, JJ taught his younger brothers. They also followed in each other's footsteps and quit school early to work in seasonal construction and earn enough money to buy their first car. When construction shut down for the winter, they repaired other people's vehicles for money. Their hands were stained from motor oil and blistered from the construction work. The Havonick family was renowned for their helpfulness, for making every effort to lend a hand to anyone who asked.

When Darren married Malinda's sister, he bought a house and had it moved next to the homestead. About six years later, he inherited his father's misfortune and was diagnosed with Multiple

Sclerosis as well. Also like his dad, he was addicted to alcohol and cigarettes. His weakening body consumed most of his attention. When his disability prevented him from working, he became irritable and abusive toward his wife and children. A few years later his wife left with the two children. Darren then lived alone in the emptiness of his house. He drank more and bitter feelings about his divorce festered. His disease seemed to attack his body more rapidly; to the point where he could barely steady his hands long enough to bring food to his mouth. He sank into a deep depression and wallowed in self-pity about how he was destined to spend the rest of his life in a wheelchair, like his father, dependent upon others for his every need. When Cathy was old enough to drive, she visited regularly and helped him with whatever he needed. Ten days before her twenty-second birthday Darren put an end to his difficulties. With a single gun shot wound to his head, he was found dead on the living room floor in a pool of his blood.

The funeral was in the local Roman Catholic Church which was renowned for its characteristic splendour. It preserved the aroma of frankincense from over one hundred years of use; the scent penetrated every fibre of its masterful structure. Rows of arched stained glass windows paraded the walls and radiated beams of vibrant colours onto the pews. Above, hand-painted murals covered every inch of the domed ceiling. The acoustics were outstanding; the music from the hymns and the musical instruments resounded in a way that was second to none in the diocese. The steeple that reached high above all other roofs housed a one ton brass bell. A big woven rope hung from its housing all the way down to the floor by the front entrance to the church.

At the funeral, Darren's twelve year old nephew served as an altar boy. He waited at the entrance for the priest to give a signal for him to ring the bell. When the time came, he clenched the rope with both hands and applied all his body weight to put it in motion. With every tug, the bell increased its swaying momentum until a series of reverberating dongs echoed throughout the region. That signified that Mass would start in fifteen minutes.

Malinda took the few remaining minutes to get some inner peace. She closed her eyes and imagined the song she was about to sing looked like musical notes reaching up to heaven. When she opened her eyes she noticed her two daughters had arrived and were sitting with their stepfather, Malinda's second husband. The pews were quickly filling with young and old. Malinda looked at them and spotted the first man she married. She forgot that he would likely attend the funeral. Being in the same place with Richard as well as her former two husbands would normally have made Malinda locate the nearest exit and tactfully cut her presence short. She fought the urge to do so and reset her focus to inner peace. She closed her eyes but instead of finding tranquility, she thought, *I had two husbands and I am living with Richard. I don't want to spend the rest of my life with him.* Malinda zoomed to the very depth of her heart and thought, *I have failed at finding love.* At that moment, the church bell stopped ringing. Malinda opened her eyes and saw more people walking in. Other than the odd cough or child murmuring, it was awfully quiet. Like a movie reel inside her mind, a playback of memories began to depict her life as her past, present and future merged together.

Escape to the Woodlands

Malinda was born in the early fifties at which time she had five older siblings. Because the children had to go to an English Protestant school her mother was adamant about moving to the French Catholic Parish of St. Agnes where both she and her husband were from. Malinda's grandfather on her mother's side was an immigrant from France. Malinda's mother had difficulty speaking English and was concerned about abandoning her cultural roots. When Malinda was just a baby, her family left a well-established dairy farm and set up anew in Ste. Agnes. They lived one mile outside of town on three hundred and sixty acres of dense poplar forestland. Brush was cleared for the homestead yard and a well was dug. Relatives formed a working bee to open more land for crop fields and pastures. The soil was stony and several large boulders had to be dug out of the ground and piled together at the center and edges of the field. When that was done they built a barn. The livestock and machinery were first to be relocated to the new site. A chicken coop was moved from the previous farm. Malinda's mother cleaned it up and made it into a home. She used curtains to divide three separate bedrooms. There was one room for the three boys and another for Malinda and her two older sisters. Plumbing and electricity were installed and the family settled in. Two years later another girl was born.

Three years after the move, the working bee gathered together once again and built a beautiful and spacious house. It had the luxuries of hot water and a flushing toilet that the previous house did not have. Its primary heat source was a home made wood burning barrel furnace located in the basement and a large wood burning cook stove in the kitchen. After everything was ready, the family moved in and the parish priest blessed the new house.

After a few years, more land was cleared and Malinda's father bought more cattle. The barn was upgraded with a bulk tank installed to keep the milk cool until a transfer truck picked it up and transported it to the city. Once a year the family went to the city park where the dairy company hosted a farmer's picnic. They participated in games, ate free ice cream and visited the city zoo. Locally, the family went to baseball tournaments and parish fundraising events at the parish hall for amusement.

The forest on and around the farm was a paradise filled with delight for Malinda. When she was ten, one of her favorite pastimes was to follow a cow path behind the barn and see where it would lead to. The farm dog took it upon himself to escort her on the trails where nature and its surroundings never disappointed her. Encircled above her was a ceiling made of blue skies and richness of a bright yellow sun sometimes surrounded by white puffy clouds. Creation existed in the wonders of its own beautiful state where hours of adventure went by like minutes. Malinda marvelled at how this habitat could survive without any help from humans. In its magnificence this world extended an intuitive expression of welcome. During her visits in the farmland meadows and forest, Malinda encountered many small animals. The butterflies, bees, ladybugs, grasshoppers, birds and squirrels made wonderful companions for her.

The beauty of the outdoors was not only seen by Malinda, but could also be heard. The tall trees reverberated and swayed to the rhythm of the branches as they danced with every gust of wind. Wildflowers added to the festivities with an assortment of rich colors and perfumes. Along the cow path were many playthings, like a branch fallen from a tree that made a wand which Malinda held to make her feel like a powerful princess. At the touch of her rod, she imagined that anything was possible and the role to defend and protect from harm the peace of the land was her given assignment. Preserving the forest's tranquil existence was her purpose. In this land, singing was the communication of choice. Malinda made up songs and dedicated them to her forest companions. A studio for the melodies emerged while Malinda belted out her songs to the trees, the animals and the sky above.

One day during a stroll into the forest, she stooped down to observe an anthill and watched the scores of tiny insects scurry about very busy with tasks. She became curious about what went on inside the mound and poked through the hill with her stick.

With one slice down the middle it seemed like a trillion ants rushed out in frenzy. Each one participated in a rescue mission and immediately began to repair and to rebuild the colony. Some moved soil to fix the damaged structure while others relocated eggs to a safer section inside the mound. Malinda watched the process for several minutes and saw something other than the physical attributes that these little creatures displayed. The ants showed no revenge toward her. They didn't get mad at her.

Malinda's home was not as peaceful as the forest. Her mother continued to have more children. Malinda was the sixth of eleven children and she shared a bedroom now with four younger siblings. The youngest was a baby that slept in a crib beside her parents' bed. There was a 'pecking order' among the children. The older siblings bossed the younger ones around and used sarcasm and teasing to trouble them. Not a day went by without some type of conflict between some of the children. As in every family, each child had his or her own unique personality. Some were passive and played quietly while others were rambunctious and loud. Malinda found solace in the forest.

Malinda's mother had the features of her descendants from France. She was short with dark wavy hair and deep brown eyes. She had only a grade six education but that fact was not an indication of her intellect. She was a loyal wife and committed to her religion. She would say, "If I had it my way, I would not have had so many children." But she and her husband obeyed the religious doctrine to have as many children as possible in spite of her view on the subject. She happily pioneered the Catholic Women's League of the parish in Ste. Agnes. She was generally passive and quiet. She tended to the piles of laundry that her large family produced and cooked three hefty meals a day for them. She tended a one half acre of vegetable garden and supplied the family with enough canned food to last the entire winter. She was a talented seamstress and made her own patterns by choosing a style on a model in the Eaton's catalogue. Every afternoon she retreated to her bedroom for a rest where she read and did crossword puzzles. After a full day of domestic tasks she liked to sit in her rocking chair to mend or knit socks, scarves, toques and mittens. Other hobbies included playing the fiddle and number painting.

Malinda's father was tall and thin with large hands that were callused from toil. Some of his fingers were stained from rolling and smoking tobacco cigarettes. He had blue eyes and auburn hair which he began to lose prematurely in his mid twenties. He obtained a diploma in agriculture through a college run by Trappist Monks in the city. He was proficient in welding, mechanics, carpentry, butchering and meat cutting. He married young and became a pillar in his community. He held positions of director for the church syndicate and was elected district municipal councillor. At home he held the traditional role of breadwinner and was cautious with money but spared no expense to assure the family had plenty to eat. He worked hard and worried much. His rules conformed to his religion. At times he was stressed and got unusually angry.

Built in the center of town were an elementary school, convent, rectory and a church. This nucleus was the focal point of the community. Behind these structures were an outdoor skating rink and a baseball diamond with a modest kiosk. At the turn of the century the first school was built on an acre of land purchased from one of the homeowners. The school was blessed by a Bishop. All the parents helped. Some by supplying cordwood, some by helping with the annual cleaning and some by joining different work bees. A teacher was hired and a nearby resident was paid a small salary to light the fire in the stove and bring drinking water. The project was funded by donations and volunteer work. Each family helped by providing a certain amount of lumber and donated specific hours of work time. More families moved into the area and student enrolment increased and outgrew the one room school house. Another school was built beside the existing one. The parishioners and their priest persevered in their request that the Sisters of Saint-Joseph start a mission in Ste. Agnes. A convent was built and two nuns took over the teaching duties. Grades five to eight were in the new school and grades one to four remained in the old school. Each building housed about thirty students in four grades.

Malinda started school with children one year older than she was. At four years of age she was registered in grade one since there was no kindergarten. She walked one mile with her older siblings and her cousins who lived a half-mile up the road.

There was always a pot of simmering homemade soup on the stove for after school. There was time to play while the family waited for their father to come in for supper. The family shared a meal of mother's French cooking know-how. After dinner the parents retreated to the living room and watched the local news on television. The older girls washed the mountain of dishes and swept the kitchen floor. Then it was milking time and the older boys went to the barn with their father.

Each night before bedtime, Malinda's father called the family to the kitchen where everyone knelt to recite the rosary. After which her mother stoked the furnace and cook stove with wood. Then, ten o'clock, seven days a week, was bedtime.

Just as the daily routines were foreseeable, Christmas took on its predictable characteristics. It started one month prior with baking to prepare for the biggest family dinner of the year held immediately after Midnight Mass. The first to be made was a dark fruitcake rich with a careful mixture of nuts, dried fruits, red and green sugared cherries, dates and molasses. After it was baked and cooled, Malinda watched her mother wrap the fruitcake snugly with a cloth and wax paper. Then she put it in the fridge. This allowed the various flavours to intermingle. A couple of days before Christmas the mother resumed their traditional baking and filled the house with sweet aromas from a variety of homemade pies and a large matrimonial cake. These were placed in a tiered platter and safely tucked away from the children on top of the fridge. Even with all that baking there was always time made to knead a batch of home made bread. Later when the first grandchildren were born, a dozen mini dinner rolls were made just for them. A sweet delight called *sucre-à-crème* topped the list of baking favourites. Its literal translation, 'creamed sugar', was accurate because its three ingredients consisted of brown sugar, fresh dairy cream and butter. Malinda's mother stirred the treat carefully in a pot on the stove just enough to form a perfect consistency of soft fudge. When the peanuts were added, the mixture was poured onto a flat cooking sheet and left to cool before being sliced into one-inch squares. Malinda's mother also bought Christmas candies to add colour and fun to the festive season.

At school, Christmas was a cherished time also. Sister Superior warned the students that when making Christmas cards for their parents, drawings of Santa Claus were strictly forbidden.

On one particular Friday afternoon, Malinda's card was ready for the final touch. The children glued small amounts of white sugar on their pictures to create the effect of sparkling snow. Malinda drew a picture of a house with a big wreath on the door and a snow man with a candy cane in his mouth. She gave it to her mother and watched for her reaction. Malinda's mother returned the card and said, "You can hang it with the rest of the cards in the living room." Several cards received in the mail hung on a string slung across the front of the fake fireplace. Santa Claus was not boycotted at home and Malinda placed her card beside one that had a large picture of the jolly old man's chubby cheerful face.

The school curriculum added the story of Jesus' birth and sang Christmas hymns. Malinda attentively listened to the story as she associated it with the plastic figurines that her mother displayed on top of the fireplace. Her mother let Malinda play with the set. Although the kings were rich and adorned with jewels, fine clothes and held gifts of gold, Malinda's favorite characters that visited Baby Jesus were the shepherds. She envied their lifestyle of spending their days savouring the luxuries of nature. They played music on stringed instruments and flutes. Their audience was their flock of sheep. They get to cuddle soft lambs rather than the large stinky cows that Malinda's family had on the farm, she thought.

Not all school memories were pleasant as one day when Malinda was in second grade; Sister Superior entered the classroom and announced that they were going to the cemetery. The school emptied as the students formed a straight line outside. Malinda's home room teacher, Sister Antoinette led the group. Sister Superior walked behind to ensure that the children behaved properly. During the march, talking and fooling around were not allowed. They walked past the convent and the rectory to the cemetery gate behind the church. They entered and gathered in the center of all the tombstones in front of a life- sized monument of Jesus nailed to a wooden cross. Sister Superior told the children to notice the lovely white picket fence that encircled the cemetery. She then led the children to the southern corner and pointed to an unmarked grave on the other side of the fence and said, "The man buried there is separated from the Christian graves because he never went to church. If he had attended confession at least once during Lent and had attended church on Easter Sundays, he would not have been excommunicated." Hearing the word 'excommunicated' for the first time frightened Malinda.

That year a new school was built to replace both of the old ones. Malinda's father was Secretary-treasurer for the St. Agnes School District and shared the responsibility of having the new two-room school built. This time, the building contract was given to a construction company. There was no work bee but some local residents were hired. Electricity, running water and flushing toilets were installed. To allow room for the new building, one of the older schools was sold to one of the residents who used the lumber to build his house.

The new structure housed two classrooms and bathrooms. A lounge with a small kitchenette and a bathroom only for the nuns were built into the plans. The old beat-up double student desks with attached benches were gone and new single desks and chairs were purchased. They gleamed with the varnished natural wood which they were made from. In each of the two classrooms was a single pedestal that held a large matching desk and chair for the teaching nun. The faded blackboards were also gone and replaced with two walls of new green chalkboards. There were no more squeaky wooden floorboards. The light green vinyl tiles shimmered from their first coats of liquid wax. The school trustees and educators received government grants for their school and were proud and boasted about the success of the project.

Sister Superior lay down a series of warnings as she instructed, "Your desks and chairs must never be written on or have the least little scratch on them. Also, important officials from the city called school inspectors will pay us two separate visits. English inspectors will make one visit. When they are here, hide your French books and speak only English. When the French inspectors arrive, you can speak French and you don't have to hide any books."

The first time the English officials made a surprise visit was on a morning, just a few minutes after the start of the school day, right after morning prayers. They drove up in an expensive-looking car and wore suits. Everyone got nervous, even Sister Superior. The strangers made their way to the front door. Sister Superior said to both classes, "The inspectors are here! Put away your French books and scribblers. Hide them deep inside your desks. Don't speak French." On her way out, she gave the children a serious look and said, "Be on your best conduct." She let the two men in and had a brief conversation with them. She gave them a tour of their new school starting with the girls' and boys' bathrooms and the teachers' lounge. Malinda hid her French textbooks and put a couple of English books on top of them. The officials went into Sister Superior's class and then into Malinda's classroom. They walked up and down the aisles and admired the condition of the student desks. Then they sat at the back of the classroom and observed the teaching of a lesson; and finally, they walked beside each desk to take a peek at the children's work. Malinda could hear her heart beat fast and loudly. The consequence of pulling out a French book, even accidentally, was never explained but Malinda was sure the consequence would be the worst punishment in the history of the school. Around noon the men left and Malinda was glad to see them go.

The following year, Sister Sainte-Antoinette was no longer there. Malinda was disappointed when Sister Superior introduced a different nun who would teach the class. The new nun never smiled. At times she disciplined the children harshly. One day during a morning recess, Malinda and her friends were skipping rope when a fourth grader ran to them. He was out of breath and shouted, "Come see! Theophil! He's tied up and he's really mad!" Theophil was Malinda's younger cousin who had just started school. Malinda immediately dropped the skipping rope. She followed the messenger back to the classroom where she found several students crowded together at the doorway. Then she heard a scream. She pushed her way in and saw Theophil bound to his chair with tape as he struggled violently to get loose. The nun stood beside him and had a pair of scissors in her hand. She told Theophil that if he sat still for five minutes, she would cut him free. Theophil remained stubborn and screeched obscenities at her. The nun was scolding Theophil because he was fidgeting and could not sit still. The boy had a constant twitch that he could not control. He was detained during recess in spite of his condition. When he was not allowed to play outside with the other kids, he got angry and the nun tied him up with a roll of white medical tape she found in the first aid kit. "Let me go, you stupid cow," he cussed. He got slapped a couple of times across the face and was put on exhibition for the other children to see. Malinda was furious with the new nun but she could not say or do anything. No one dared to interfere. Malinda missed Sister Antoinette.

Later that year, Malinda had difficulty concentrating and neglected her schoolwork. As a result she failed grade three. The following year Malinda repeated the grade. One thing good about failing was that she was the same age as the rest of her new peers. She and a girl named Lorraine became best friends. The two were inseparable. In grade five they moved to the classroom next door with sixth, seventh and eighth graders. The classroom was divided in half; boys on one side and girls on the other. Any sort of contact with the opposite sex was disallowed. At the back of the room where the children hung their coats, the girls' clothes hanger area was separate from the boys'. Sister Superior often used physical force to discipline the children and gave out lots of homework assignments. She said it was to prepare them for grade nine at a high school in a larger town twelve miles away. "The years at high school would be more difficult than the elementary years," said the nun.

Children in grades five through eight were expected to pray longer and more frequently. There was the Morning Prayer before classes began. After the lunch hour recess the students knelt beside their desks to recite the rosary. This ritual consisted of recitation of the Apostles' Creed followed by the Lord's Prayer, then several small acknowledgements and fifty Hail Marys. Sister Superior began the prayer time with the order, "Close your eyes and bow your heads." During one of those occasions, the prayers were interrupted by the sound of Sister Superior walking up to Lorraine and shouting, "Your eyes were not closed!" Lorraine was kneeling with her head bowed. She murmured, "If you had yours closed, then how come you could see me?" Malinda thought that her friend was about to receive a beating so she said a quick prayer to God that Lorraine would be spared from a whipping. Sister Superior slapped Lorraine on the back of her head once. She did nothing more than that.

Along with the regular curriculum the students were taught an added subject that extended the regular school day by an extra half-hour to end at four o'clock. The children learned about the doctrines of the church in a Roman Catholic booklet entitled

"Catechism." Also, the children were appointed church duties. The boys were commissioned to serve during mass as altar boys. The parish priest taught their functions and procedures. The girls' lot was to sing. They gave up most of their lunch hour recesses to meet with the music teacher at the church for choir practice. Malinda and Lorraine were resentful that the boys got to enjoy playing sports during that time, so they plotted to disrupt the singing group in order to get kicked out of the session. Their plan worked well and they headed to the convent for a visit with the housekeeping nun whom they befriended. The girls were invited inside for milk and cookies. They did not bother to admit their offence to Sister Superior as they were told to do. When recess was over and the school bell rang, the two waited for the other choirgirls to pass by the convent in order to rejoin the group and walk back to school together. Eventually the two unauthorized guests were caught and they stood in front of Sister Superior waiting for their reprimand. Sister Superior called the girls into the teachers' lounge. She first addressed Lorraine. While pointing a finger at her, she said, "Malinda is a bad influence on you and you should not be friends with her." To Malinda she said, "You will stay after school beginning today for an extra half hour until Christmas break." She phoned both the girls' parents and reported her decision. For Malinda this meant a penance of two months, but she did not fear it as much as she feared what her father might do to her. Malinda arrived home just a few minutes after her father came in for supper. Her father was silent throughout dinner. Malinda expected that he would explode in anger at any moment, but there was only the sound of cutlery scraping against dinner plates. The only spoken words were when someone asked that a dish of food be passed. Everyone ate in silence. Before Malinda got home, there had been talk about what she and Lorraine had done. Malinda's father finished his dessert and said, "It's always the older ones who cause trouble and give a bad example to the others." Malinda's body twitched in fear of what might happen next. However, she did not receive the smacking she expected. Instead she experienced an indelible imprint of the shameful words both her father and Sister Superior said about her.

The next day of school was a Monday when Sister Superior called Malinda to stand beside her pedestal and face the class to recite a four-verse poem, which had been assigned as weekend homework. Malinda could only remember the first two lines correctly. Sister Superior opened the top drawer of her desk and took out a leather honing strap and commanded, "Hold out your right hand, palm up." Malinda received four hits of the strap, then the nun said, "You'll come to my desk again tomorrow and recite the entire poem correctly." That evening after supper dishes were done, Malinda spent an hour memorizing the poem. That night she slept restlessly, fearful that she would forget the words. Lack of sleep made her tired the next day. When Sister Superior called her to the front, Malinda was able to recite the first two verses before making a mistake. The same outcome occurred. A couple of days went by without being called to the front. On Friday, when Malinda was summoned to the front, she recited the poem in its entirety without error. Much to her surprise, Sister Superior said, "Repeat the poem to me and include the punctuation marks." Malinda could not meet the challenge and she was given two more whacks with the strap. She was told to return to her seat and the ordeal ended without further reproach.

Mass also had its share of episodes. Mass was conducted in Latin and the congregation did not understand the language; however, the priest delivered a ten-minute sermon in French. Eventually mass was conducted in the language of the people. A little booklet was designed to facilitate comprehension. Its monthly publication was distributed to the congregation. In it were the upcoming masses for the period with every word and theme of each mass. The Parish received a year's supply at a time.

In spite of the changes, Malinda and Lorraine lost interest in church and asked their parents if they could sit together in a pew away from their families. When they received permission they chatted and giggled throughout the service. The church custodian approached the girls and scolded them, but the more they tried to stop giggling the more they did. The next day when the girls arrived at school, they saw their names written with giant letters that covered one entire chalkboard. They knew they were in deep trouble. After Morning Prayer, Sister Superior lectured the girls and told the class that never since the school opened in the 1930's, had there been such disruptive girls as these two. Malinda and Lorraine both received after school detention until they finished doing a major cleaning of the library books, windows, blinds and all the walls.

Malinda no longer liked school. At the start of term in September, she looked forward longingly to the Christmas holidays when she would be free from Sister Superior's ordinances. Since her liberation was accredited to the birth of Christ, Malinda made sure she thanked Jesus for the break.

A woman from the congregation gave birth to a baby girl who lived for only a few hours. The infant was not given a church funeral. She was buried outside the cemetery fence beside the pagan grave. At school, when the children asked Sister Superior why, she said, "Because the baby was not baptized." The explanation did not sit right with Malinda. It reminded her of the teaching about when Jesus was among a crowd of people and the adults kept the children at bay and told them not to bother the rabbi. Only the adults stood close to him. When they took the children away, Jesus said, "Let the little ones come to me." Malinda could not bring herself to believe that God would not accept the infant girl that died shortly after birth and began to question the strict religion of her parents which was, in her view, the reason they had so many children. She saw poverty in some of the larger families that her classmates came from and thought; *when I get married I'm not going to live like my mother does.* Malinda questioned if the practice was not just a method of guaranteeing the existence of the Catholic structure. When she doubted the doctrines of her faith and the validity of certain religious customs, she felt guilty.

When Malinda compared her family with those of the community she found it to be more financially successful than most others; however, it was not excluded from the stresses of a large family. Sometimes Malinda's father got extremely angry. On many occasions she witnessed her father use a wooden plank to smack a cow across its back when it would not get into its stall. Other times he would poke an unruly cow with a pitchfork. His rages demonstrated physical abuse, coarse language and lengthy complaints about the stupidity of the animal along with utterances about money. Anything that displeased him could trigger his rages. Sometimes he beat his teenage sons. Although Malinda did not witness him ever using a weapon on the boys, her father's behavior was a replicate of his rages during an attack on one of the cows. On a certain Saturday evening, Hubert was watching his favourite Saturday night hockey game on TV. His father told him to shut the TV off for the nightly prayers. Hubert only turned the volume down. Then he knelt at the kitchen entrance from where he could see the TV. During prayers he watched TV and was so consumed in the game that he did not notice that the prayers suddenly stopped, nor did he hear his father's footsteps rapidly approaching. His father struck him across the head several times with an open hand and blasphemed obscenities at him. Hubert protected his head with his arms, remained kneeling and said nothing. Family members avoided looking at what was happening but Malinda watched with indignation. Then her father returned to his kneeling position at the table and resumed the prayers. There were other times when his father using a closed fist beat Hubert about the face. Malinda was horrified to see blood flow from her brother's face. The hits were always accompanied with verbal criticisms of disapproval. Hubert was not the first to receive beatings. Malinda had seen the same thing happen to an older brother.

One afternoon Malinda's father and Hubert entered the house carrying a heavy cardboard box, which had a piece of machinery in it. Malinda went to see what was happening. They were at the top of the basement staircase when Malinda heard her father say to her brother, "Don't rip the box." Her father carried one end of the box and headed backwards down each step of the staircase. Hubert held the other end but with difficulty because he had to bend down to hold the box at the other end. The corner of the box that he was holding ripped. Immediately his father snapped and said, "You ripped the box on purpose!" Hubert rebutted, "I had to grab it there. The box was slipping out of my hands and it would have fallen on you." They managed to carry the box the rest of the way. Malinda heard her father badger her brother all the way up the staircase. Hubert was about to go outside when his father grabbed him and turned him around. Her father hit Hubert on the nose and blood was all over his face. Hubert retorted, "Come on! Hit me again! Hit!" Her brother received more blows to the face. It seemed like this beating would never end. Suddenly Malinda's mother yelled from the kitchen, "If you don't stop hitting him, I'm going to call the police!" At the sound of those words, Malinda wanted to cheer. The beating stopped abruptly. Malinda was happy never to see her father hit her brother again, but she was unaware of the beatings that occurred away from family members.

When the last of Malinda's older siblings left home, she was afraid of becoming her father's next target so she tried to get on his good side. There seemed to be no pleasing him. Her father often called the younger sister to help but he would not ask Malinda. When she asked to help him, he would refuse the offer. Most times he simply would not answer her until one night, she got tired of her father's aloofness and took it upon herself to show up for the milking. She stood in the center of the alley way and waited for her father to finish supervising one of the cows being milked by an automated machine. He pulled the suction device off the cow and opened the steel container attached to the machine. Malinda walked over to an empty steel pail that her father put in the alley. He poured the milk in the bucket and said, "Bring this to the milk house and empty it in the bulk tank." Malinda exclaimed with enthusiasm and with confidence, she said, "Okay!" She waited beside the pail while her father poured the milk. When she saw that he filled it to the bucket's rim, Malinda quickly lost her confidence. With both hands firmly clenched on the handle she could only lift the pail slightly off the cement floor. She trudged along taking one tiny step after another, holding the pail between her legs. She made her way down the alley to the manure drainage gutter which she had to step over in order to get to the milk house. She set the pail down. With a deep breath, she took the handle again and put one foot on the other side of the gutter. It was only about a foot or so wide. She stepped over this passage a trillion times in the past without thinking about it but all of a sudden, it seemed like it was a huge gorge. When she brought her other foot across, the bucket hooked the edge of the gutter. Malinda lost her balance and fell. She lay partly in the gutter surrounded by spilled milk. Her father heard the noise and he headed toward her. When he saw what happened, he shouted, "You just spilled dollars of milk, you good for nothing! Get out of here! Go!" As Malinda ran out of the barn she looked behind to see if her father was following but he remained in the barn. Malinda thought, *maybe he'll beat me later.*

Belonging Somewhere

Behind the school playground was an outdoor community sports area. It had a skating rink, two baseball diamonds, two outhouses, a concession stand and a three-tier sitting structure for the fans. The town's work bee built all the structures. A male adult and a junior boys team belonged to a district baseball league. Every Sunday after church Malinda's family went home to have a quick lunch and to change their clothes. Her mother packed sandwiches and other foods for the day in a cardboard box. The family piled into the car and headed out to wherever the baseball games were being hosted in one of the nearby towns. Once they arrived, Malinda's father gave each child twenty-five cents to spend at the canteen. Malinda would save her quarter for later in the day when she would buy her favourite treat, a box of caramel popcorn and an orange pop.

When Malinda was 12, the district league approved a women's league. Lorraine's father organized a team that included his two daughters and Malinda. The men's team donated some of their old equipment to get the girls started. Lorraine's father worked his teen girls team very hard and gave them one hundred percent commitment. By the end of the first season, the team was the best in the league and won the playoffs. The team was given a cash reward which the coach used to purchase uniforms for the girls' next season. The following year the girls were highly motivated to begin their baseball season. With their striking new uniforms colored yellow, white and black, they gave all they had when they competed. The second year's reward bought them new equipment. Each year, bringing the trophy home rewarded their efforts.

The sport forced Lorraine and Malinda to make new friends as they cheered and encouraged each other. This made the two girls appreciate and know the other girls on the team. Baseball became Malinda's new passion. It did not matter what time she had to get up to wait for Lorraine's father to pick her up for a tournament. One of the towns was an hour's drive away. Malinda had to get up at 5:00 a.m. to be ready. The more the girls won, the more games they had to play. Sometimes the weather would not cooperate. On rainy days the games were cancelled but all other times the sport was on, even in temperatures that rose to eighty or ninety degrees Fahrenheit. Sometimes they fought heavy winds or hordes of mosquitoes. At times they had to play four or five games in a day. None of that mattered to Malinda. She loved the sport and because of it she had a sense of belonging somewhere. Her dad never came to watch their games but her mother socialized with the other parents and cheered the team on.

In the midst of her baseball enthusiasm, Malinda graduated from elementary school and was bussed to Youville where she attended her first year of high school. Malinda was fairly familiar with the town because of the baseball tournaments, which were occasionally hosted there. Malinda soon got to know the town better. She marvelled at the fact it had more than one grocery store, a lumberyard and a hardware store. The town also boasted a bakery, a bank, a furniture store and several other businesses. The sports area had a large arena that was heated. There were three restaurants, one medical clinic with access to three doctors and a hospital. It even had a movie theatre, which Malinda wanted to go to someday. The church building was huge compared to the one in Ste. Agnes. Its steeple could be seen for miles around. The main streets were paved and had sidewalks of cement blocks.

Malinda and Lorraine enjoyed the twelve-mile bus ride to Youville. The roads were dusty and bumpy but the girls did not mind at all. They got to be together for an entire hour there and back. The high school was much larger than the tiny two-room one in Ste. Agnes. It was two storeys high and had many classrooms. There was a significantly large gymnasium just for the high school students. Another wing was attached to the school, which was for the elementary students of Youville. They had their own gym. The schoolyard was the size of two football fields. The two girls immediately got involved in track and field, basketball and volleyball.

The principal was Sister Clucier. She wore a different habit than the nuns did at St. Agnes School. She belonged to a different

Order of Nuns and did not have a saint's name. She was talented at directing the school choir, the largest in the province because it consisted of every student in her high school. The group was renowned for its presentation and ability to harmonize alto, soprano and bass voices in such grand songs as "Climb Every Mountain." The girls wore the school uniform that was a grey tunic and a white blouse. The boys wore black or grey dress pants with a white shirt and for the performances, they wore a tie. Sometimes the choir was invited to perform at important events and traveled by bus to other communities. Their show received applause and praise.

Sister Clucier was short-tempered. She stood over six feet tall and when she was upset, her eyes would enlarge and the whites of her eyes seemed to inflate. She picked on certain boys, especially one named Gilbert. His bangs were long and parted on the side and they covered part of his face. He was a reserved fellow who smoked marijuana every day. He was a friendly introvert and had no enemies. It was the sixties and Gilbert fit the profile of a real hippie.

Gilbert came to school one day with an injured foot. The doctor told him not to put too much pressure on that leg. Sister Clucier had a rule that required everyone to stand tall and straight during choir practice. During the weekly practice, Gilbert put his weight on the good leg while standing. Sister Clucier did not put up with that and told him to stand straight. Gilbert swayed from side to side in an attempt to relieve pressure on his injury. Then Sister Clucier told him to stand beside her. Gilbert limped and arrived beside her. That was when she flung three slaps back and forth on each side of his head. The choir stood still as though feeling his pain. Sister Clucier made him stand straight on both his legs while remaining beside her for the remainder of the practice. She resumed directing the choir. The students sang with a lump in their throat from watching Gilbert with sweat on his forehead and his hair all messed up.

A few weeks after the Gilbert incident, Sister Clucier arrived at school with a cast on one of her legs and walked with crutches. She did not explain how her accident happened. That day she appointed Mr. Farris to be acting principal during her leave of absence. He was an African American who taught university preparation level history and literature. He was tall and his eyes also bulged out when he was angry but he was not violent.

The staff now consisted of 'ordinary' men and women except for one other nun, Sister Bernadette. She belonged to another different order of nuns. Her habit was a blue tunic with a white blouse with no headwear. She taught French grammar and literature. She was a young, petite woman with lots of energy. Her personality was stable and her smile reflected joy. She loved music and introduced songs of francophone pop artists within the French program. Her students got to go on outings such as a weekend retreat to meet other francophone students from throughout the province. Sister Bernadette was Malinda's homeroom teacher.

High school was fun and not at all what Sister Superior forewarned. There was significantly less homework and hardly any on the weekends. There were neither catechism classes nor choir practices during recess time. The days of a gender segregated classroom were over. There were teens from surrounding towns as well as those of Youville. Malinda's grade nine classes consisted of twenty-nine students, just as many as the total of the four grade classes in Ste. Agnes. During the course of their first year of high school, Malinda and Lorraine expanded their friendship to include three new friends.

The girls enjoyed their first year of high school with too much frolic, unfortunately. One Monday morning near the end of the school year, Sister Bernadette announced that on Friday afternoon, the entire school would be meeting in the gym to watch a film. Normally this would be a wonderful treat, but the film was about hockey summer camp training. Since it was only the boys that were involved in hockey, several girls requested that a different film be chosen – one that suited both genders. When they were turned down, Malinda and her four friends had a conversation about a protest. It was just talk but on Friday, when the hallways of the school were filled with students and teachers on their way to the gym, Malinda and her friends walked together and grumbled about how unfairly girls were treated when it came to sports. As they advanced toward the gym, they were near a door when one of the friends named Sue said, "Come on!" She led them outside and the four girls ran and followed her. There was no time to think. Sue ran a couple of blocks to her house and the others were right behind. Sue's parents were at work and there was no one home. The girls entered and huddled in the living room around the coffee table. While catching their breath, they congratulated themselves about how they thwarted the principal's plan. After they settled down, they ate snacks and watched TV while looking at fashion magazines. There was a lot of talking and laughter until Lorraine shouted, "Malinda, our bus leaves in ten minutes!" The fun came to an end and the two girls left. They thought to make it back just in time for the school bus to arrive and make their way into the crowd of students outside. "No one will notice us," said Lorraine, but when they arrived and saw their school bus leaving, they knew that fate had a different plan for them. The bus driver radioed the principal about their absence. Mr. Farris looked for the two girls in the empty schoolyard. He spotted them walking toward the school. He stood with his arms crossed so tightly over his chest that his suit jacket crinkled upwards toward his shoulders. The girls reluctantly approached him as Mr. Farris summoned them with an unsympathetic stare. In a despondent tone he said, "Come, girls. Come with me." Feeling like little sheep being lead to slaughter, the girls quietly followed him to his office. They watched as Mr. Farris phoned Lorraine's parents. He hung up and said, "Lorraine, your dad will pick both of you up. In the meantime, both of you stand outside my office in the corridor against the wall until he gets here." The girls expected a lecture from him but he said nothing more, and the girls dared not say anything.

Lorraine's dad was furious. He was a short man with a stocky build and had a powerful voice when he shouted. This was one of the reasons he was such an effective baseball coach. His shouts to instruct and encourage carried well beyond the player in center field. On this particular day he shouted his anger and disappointment all the way home.

Malinda feared the worst when she got home; however, it seemed like her parents had no knowledge of her escapade. At the return of school on Monday morning, it was a different story. The five girls were summoned to the principal's office. Not one of the girls would disclose which ones were the instigators of the pack. Mr. Farris declared that Malinda and Sue must be the bad influence because their school grades were the lowest compared to the other three girls. Their punishment was that they would not be allowed to write their final exams. For Malinda and Sue, though the 'trial' was short-lived, the bitterness of the pill they had to swallow lasted a long time. While all the students met in the gymnasium to write their provincial exams, Malinda and Sue stood idle in the hallway.

Mr. Farris announced that Sister Clucier retired and would not return. He introduced a new principal, a man from Youville. Malinda's friends from that town knew him and did not like him, although they applauded his doing away with the school uniform regulation.

Two days before school ended for summer break, a boy from Malinda's class came to her and said, "I saw your mother leaving the principal's office. She was crying." Up to this point, Malinda had accepted her punishment as befitting her crime, but she hated that her mother was hurt. "The new principal made my mother cry?" she fumed. The boy answered, "Yeah, I saw her leave the office as she was walking to her car." Then Malinda's tone subsided as she asked, "Was my father there?" The boy answered, "No."

On the last day of school the new principal called Malinda and Sue to his office. "I met with the authorities of this school to discuss your behavior. I wanted both of you permanently expelled from this school, but because no girl has ever been expelled, the trustees decided to spare you from this outcome. The fact remains that you will repeat grade nine next year. I give you this warning: should there be the slightest incident of misconduct from either of you next year, you will be expelled immediately."

While riding the bus home that day, Malinda hardly said anything to Lorraine other than how her dad was going to be mad at her. She kept quiet and stared out the window most of the way. So far her father had been strangely silent. Malinda thought that maybe her mother kept the incident from him. However, failing a grade could not be concealed. Malinda said to Lorraine, "I'm going to stay out of trouble next year."

That evening during dinner, Malinda sat at the very end of the long bench against the wall with her youngest siblings. She wanted to be as far away from her father as possible. The meal proceeded as usual. Malinda thought, *maybe he doesn't know anything about this!* But when he finished his dinner, he looked down toward his empty plate and said, "It's always the older ones that cause trouble." After this cold declaration, he got up from the table and went to the living room as usual.

Escape to Isolation

September arrived and for the first time in six years, Malinda was separated from Lorraine at school. Lorraine moved on to grade ten and began to date a boy from Youville. She spent every recess with him. Malinda had counted on being with Lorraine on the bus, but eventually both girls got involved in different interests. Malinda was on the basketball team and remained after school for practices and games. She was also elected to represent grade nine on the social committee. Her new classmates were a rambunctious bunch that totalled forty-two in all. The teachers had difficulty handling them. A few of them hung around with delinquent school dropouts from Youville. They wore oversized red and black toughie shirts, worn out denim jackets and jeans. They all smoked tobacco cigarettes. When they partied, they smoked marijuana, drank beer and dropped acid. One of their pranks was to turn their school desks around to face the back of the classroom. Before the teacher arrived, the boys would mess up the entire classroom. They threw pencils, erasers and rulers at each other. Some even wrestled. The girls were known to be sexually active and also partied. Only six hard-working students remained outside this circle. Malinda tried to resist them but eventually her weakened will and efforts to behave failed. After some time she joined the clowning around. She and others were often kicked out of class to stand in the hallway by the door. When the principal walked the hallways and spotted them, he called them to his office for a lecture but never followed through with the threat to expel Malinda.

At home, Malinda's father showed no interest in her life. His aloofness made her act like a puppy starved for praise. Malinda thought to be a disappointment to her father. She introduced him to her new friends but he paid no attention to them. She dated a boy from Youville who was well mannered and had a good reputation. One evening he drove to Malinda's house. When his car pulled into the yard, all Malinda's younger siblings ran to the window to see who it was. When he knocked on the door, Malinda invited him in to meet her parents. She took his hand and led him to the living room. All the siblings followed them. "Mom, Dad, this is Tommy," she said. Her mother looked up and said, "Hello," then continued with her knitting. Her father did not look in their direction; neither did he say anything. He watched TV as though nothing was happening. Malinda stood for a moment as she waited for a shrug or a nod but his only response was a painful silence. Malinda turned to Tommy and said, "Well, let's go." Malinda pretended that nothing was wrong and was glad that Tommy never asked why her father did not greet him.

Every attempt Malinda made to change her father's opinion of her failed. She attended a cousin's wedding with the rest of her family and sat with her parents and a bunch of her father's relatives. One of them was a nun named Aunt Alma. The eldest of her father's siblings, she was tall and her habit was white with a large bleeding heart embroidered at the chest. Her headwear was also white and made her appear even taller. She was authoritative and honorably respected by the family. The relatives engaged in their normal chatter until Aunt Alma asked Malinda's father a question that no one else dared to ask. "What are you doing for help on the farm since your older boys are now moved out?" she inquired. Malinda's father replied, "I'm left with a bunch of girls. Malinda is not worth anything on the farm, but Catherine, now she drives the tractor and even my three-ton truck to get bales of hay in the field. She helps me milk cows every evening." Catherine was two years younger than Malinda. Malinda wanted to defend her case but she got up from her chair and nonchalantly pretended that she had to go to the bathroom. She managed to physically escape the experience, but she could not forget the assault on her character. The words spoken by her father that night resonated in her mind. Malinda could only conclude that her father did not like her and she did not know why.

Soon afterwards, Malinda moved to the empty bedroom in the basement that was left vacant since the older brothers moved out. The basement was a seldom-frequented place. It was cold, damp and spooky – more so at night. The bedroom was located at the far end of the basement. The only light switch for the area was at the top of the staircase. At bedtime Malinda had to shut off the basement light and find her way in the dark guided by a cinder light coming from the wood-burning furnace air valve. At times when the moon was bright, the dim shape of the woodpile beside the furnace made Malinda imagine a monster of some sort living in or behind it. Beside the woodpile was a wooden door covered in cobwebs that led to the cold storage room. To the opposite side of the squeaky furnace fan was a dark chamber made entirely of cement with a four-foot high opening that housed the well system. Once past her mother's laundry area, she had only a few more steps to make until she reached her bedroom door. Once inside, Malinda set the latch to lock and was safe from any lurking creatures prowling in the basement. Although Malinda was afraid to walk in the dark, the trip to the end of the basement was worth it. She liked that the bedroom had no window because the thieves would not frighten her. Her father believed milk was stolen from the bulk tank while everyone was asleep at night.

The bedroom was made out of plywood walls that her father built and her mother varnished. There was a student desk that had three drawers on the left that were deep and unusually wide. The set was complete with a shelving unit above. Malinda had the luxury of the entire bedroom, including a metal framed double bed, all to herself. However, to lessen her fears, she tried to have a sister share the space with her, but each of the three tried and quickly moved back upstairs. They were not as determined to dare walk in the darkness to the end of the basement even while accompanied with Malinda. In her new quarters Malinda was out-of-the-way and cut herself off from the rest of the household. Time spent in her bedroom reminded her of the woodland places she visited in years past. She sat at the student desk and drew pictures of the forest and her favourite farm animals. There was one picture she made that did not look like the rest. It portrayed a young woman standing on a round platform clothed in a fancy blouse and bellbottom pants. Malinda drew this character holding a microphone and singing to a real audience. When she finished the picture she looked at it often and dreamed that one day she would be that girl.

Upon completion of grade ten, Malinda announced to her mother that she was quitting school. Her parents were unconcerned. Malinda replied to an ad in the classified section of the city newspaper and got a job as a live-in nanny for a well-to-do Jewish family. She lied about her age to get the position. She was chosen because she was French. The mother of the household was her boss and had two preschool daughters. She wanted them to learn the French language. Malinda adapted quickly to the city and the different culture, but she soon realized that without an education, she would not get a better job. She returned home for one more year of school.

That summer she earned a total of $160. It would take every penny to purchase a lovely maroon dress from the Eaton's catalogue, along with a transistor radio and a record player with two detachable speakers. Afterwards, with the babysitting money she made, she bought some records. The music equipment was set up in her bedroom and she sang along loudly when the records played. The more she sang the more she felt a fire inside her grow. It was this passion within her that made all worries go away.

That year in school once again Malinda vowed to stay out of trouble. This time she did something different and sat in the front row of every class. It was easier to pay attention to the teaching and avoid messing around. It was hard not to take part in the schemes and practical jokes of her friends, but she persevered and her grades improved. Her classmates elected her as class president; shortly afterwards, the school body elected her to be a member of the social committee.

After Christmas break, a professional singing group from the city named "Les Cent-Noms" came to the school. They met with Sister Bernadette and the social committee. The school division agreed to hire them to promote francophone culture by recruiting high school talent throughout the province.

On a school day afternoon, Malinda showed up for the audition. She was nervous but eager to perform. Some applicants were rejected but Malinda was accepted along with a few others from her school. They were to perform at a public show that was hosted and produced by "Les Cent-Noms". Malinda could hardly wait to tell her parents. When she arrived home from school that day, she bee-lined straight to her mother and exclaimed, "Mom! I'm going to sing at the Cent-Noms show!" Her mother asked, "When's the show?"

Although Malinda regularly sang at church, this was altogether different. To sing alone on a stage and in front of an audience was just like the drawing she made in her scrapbook, except this was real. She bought herself a new outfit that looked like the one on the picture. At the live rehearsal, there were six musicians; coloured spotlights were used and a disco ball was suspended from the ceiling. Malinda sang an intense love song entitled, "Et Maintenant (What Now My Love)". It seemed her dream to have a singing career was coming true, but at times her mind drifted away from her heart and she would think, *THIS will make my dad like me.*

Malinda overheard her mother say to her father, "There is a school concert and Malinda is singing. We can go." He replied, "This family doesn't need an actress." Malinda was afraid his scorn would turn to rage toward her so she went to her room and stayed there for the rest of the evening. Malinda was determined to do whatever it took to perform, with or without her father's consent. The night of the concert, Malinda did not take the school bus home. After school she went to her friend, Sue's house. This way her father could not stop her from going.

At the event, Malinda was very surprised to see that her mother was there, though unaccompanied by her father. Malinda immediately went to her and said, "Hi. You came!" She had come with Malinda's aunt. The auditorium was filling up. It looked like they would have a full house. People came from towns around and some from outside the school division. After greeting her mother, Malinda stayed close to her friends who became her main source of confidence. Soon the manager of "Les Cent Noms" approached the microphone and announced that the event was about to begin. He called upon all the performers and asked that they sit in the first row closest to the stage. The gymnasium lights went out and three spotlights of blue, gold and red lit up the stage. The band was summoned to the stage. There were two guitarists, a keyboard player and a drummer. They played an introductory piece. Their music was loud. The excitement made Malinda happy but really nervous. After the first few performances, Malinda was introduced. She could hear her every heartbeat and her legs felt like noodles. She rose from her chair and looked at the two steps up to the stage. *I mustn't trip*, she thought. Her knees felt like they were shaking but she made it to the microphone. She wore a new ivory silk blouse and a bright pink jumpsuit skirt with an empire waist fastened with two straps that flowed over her shoulders all the way to the back. Her short blond hair hung to one side of her face while tucked behind her ear on the other side. The band played the opening chords of her number and Malinda took a deep breath. The music was intense and she sang with passion. Her knees kept shaking as she performed. When she finished, the audience applauded with great enthusiasm. *It's over!* Malinda thought. She thanked the people and headed down the steps, back to her chair. Her knees stopped trembling but she could still hear her heart beat.

When the concert was over, Malinda went to see her mother who had a crowd of people around her. Some were neighbors from Ste. Agnes but many were strangers. Malinda heard a woman say, "You're Malinda's mother? She'll go places with that voice." Her mother was delighted and agreed. Others commented with similar remarks. After the crowd dispersed, Malinda and her mother were alone. Malinda said, "Thanks for driving all the way here to make it, Mom." Her mother said, "I got this for your birthday," and gave her a tiny box. In it was a lovely wristwatch. It was the nicest present Malinda had ever received from her. Malinda's sixteenth birthday was not for a few weeks yet. She turned her heartfelt emotions toward her mother. She was happy for her mother that people sought to congratulate her. Malinda was proud that her success reflected onto her mother. She began to recognize and appreciate the support her mother gave her. Malinda had the urge to give her mother a big hug and tell her how much she loved her, but displays of affection and the words *I love you* were never used in her family.

The next day, Malinda heard her mother talk on the phone about how thrilled she was over the performance. Then she said something that Malinda never expected: "I want to send her to Toronto for singing lessons." This was a side of her mother that Malinda never knew! The overheard telephone conversation stimulated Malinda's fantasy about being a singer, but the thought of being alone in one of the biggest cities in the country began to frighten her. Then she wondered *how would mother make that possible when she has no access to money?* Malinda's father came into the kitchen to get his can of Export-A tobacco. He sat in his chair at the table and reached into his shirt pocket for his cigarette papers. While he rolled a cigarette, Malinda's mother introduced her idea to him. An argument erupted and ended quickly when her father said, "I'll hear none of that."

Malinda felt that her dream was too good to be true anyway. That night she slumped in her bed and thought about when she was five years old and her mother had taken her to a professional photographer for a photo shoot. Her mother had made ringlets of her sun-bleached locks and dressed her in a pretty blue dress that she had made of nylon material with miniscule white polka dots all over. The collar was wide and rounded and trimmed with lace. The puffed short sleeves were also trimmed with lace. Malinda wore black patent shoes with a bow on top of the strapped buckle. She sat on a light beige upholstered Victorian bench when the picture was taken. A month later her mother received the eight-by-ten inch picture along with a letter from the photographer explaining how the picture was entered into a contest and won. Her mother hung it in the living room with the other family photos. Malinda's father objected to the picture and wanted it removed from view. Malinda wanted to ask him why but dared not pose the question. Her mother took the picture down.

The next morning, Malinda's mother brought up the Toronto issue again and another argument ensued. To stop the opposition between her parents Malinda said that she did not want to go to Toronto. As a young teenager, Malinda gave up her dream.

Later, after an outing with her friends, Malinda's younger sister told her, "Father said you are a tramp." Malinda was afraid of him that day thinking that he would scold and maybe beat her, but he did nothing as though he had never said that. To appease his judgment of her, the next weekend, she once again brought her date into the house, but her parents' non-response was the same as before. She stopped dating the boy and introduced a new one in the hope that her parents would like him better. Her parents behaved the same way. Malinda thought, *I went out with nice guys and my parents did not even care.*

A high school dropout named Brian had a crush on Malinda. He hung around his own kind and the gang got into fights with rivals from the surrounding towns. Though Brian had a small build, he was brutal in a fight and used sharp objects to injure his opponent. He did drugs and drank alcohol as often as he could. He lived with his parents and did not have a job. He had a friend named JJ, one of the Havonick boys. JJ had a job in construction and owned a 'hot' car. After work, he would pick up members of the gang to search for fights and girls. They all had long dirty hair except JJ. His was clean.

To awaken her father from his lack of concern for her, Malinda decided to go out with a 'bad boy'. She befriended a classmate named Janie because she was dating one of the so-called bad boys in the gang. Janie lived in Youville and went to school dressed in a mini skirt with a hemline just below her buttocks. Her bleached blond hair was stiffened from too much colouring. Janie was known at the school as the town slut. Her demeanor was reserved and quiet but she walked with a tough attitude. Most mornings she arrived at school late and tired from her outing the night before. She often fell asleep at her desk and the teachers would often send her to the principal's office. The school counsellor ignored her and some teachers picked on her frequently without any cause. One short-tempered teacher specifically moved Janie to sit at a desk in front of the class beside his desk. The girl sat estranged from the rest of the class. Whenever this teacher's temper flared, Janie was close and he smacked her around. Janie was alone in more ways than one. She had one friend but was sent away because she was pregnant with Brian's baby.

Janie was quick to accept Malinda as a friend. When Malinda asked her mother if she could spend a weekend at Janie's house, her mother did not answer or seem to care. One cold evening, the two friends walked to the restaurant where Brian and his friends usually went to pick up girls, but the guys did not show up. Janie said, "Let's walk up and down the main street sidewalk." Malinda felt the cold biting her thighs through her jeans. Janie's legs were bare below her mini skirt. Her thighs became red and soon developed white patches on her legs. Malinda said, "this is crazy,' and insisted they head back to the house.

An hour later, Malinda was almost asleep when Janie sprung out of bed to look out the bedroom window. "What's wrong?" Malinda asked.

"It's them!" Janie replied as she changed back into her clothes.

Malinda stayed in bed and said, "It's dark; how can you tell it's them?"

Janie replied, "That's the sound of JJ's car. Come on! Let's go!" Janie was ready to go but Malinda was still in bed. "Come on Malinda, get up!" she exclaimed.

Malinda got ready and the two girls walked up and down the sidewalk again. After some time, Malinda said, "Maybe you made a mistake and it wasn't them."

"No chance! I know the sound of JJ's car," said Janie. Suddenly, a red car with loud mufflers sped past them. Janie waved at the car but it did not stop. She said, "I told you! Now we *have* to keep walking." The car went by a couple more times then it stopped.

JJ rolled down his window and said, "Are you going to stand there all night? Get in." The back door flung open and Janie's boyfriend, Paul, got out to let the girls in.

He said, "Malinda, you first." Brian was sitting at the other end of the back seat. The four sat squished together and the car sped away. Brian had his arm over the back of the seat. He smelled of cigarette smoke and alcohol.

"Do you have enough room?" he asked Malinda.

She answered, "Yeah, I'm okay."

Then Brian said, "I saw you sing at the school. I was there, you know." Malinda did not say anything.

It was past midnight when another car sped up beside them. The two cars came to a stop in the middle of the street. JJ and the other driver rolled down their windows. They knew each other. JJ challenged the other driver to a race. "I'm going to clean your clock," he said. Both drivers burned rubber and pulled power turns before they stopped one beside the other. They revved their car engines. One of the passengers from the other car got out and stood in front of and between the two cars. He counted to three and the two cars sped away. JJ won the race. During the race, Brian held Malinda tightly. "I got you," he said. "Don't be afraid." Then JJ drove to the chip stand and ordered a burger. Paul took Janie's purse and dumped everything in it on her lap. He held up a Tampax and said, "Looks like it's going to be a messy night." He took her eyebrow pencil and drew a dark brown line on her thigh all the way up to her panties. Brian was quiet. Malinda was nervous. JJ had a box of beer on the passenger front seat and offered some to everyone. Paul passed the pencil over to Brian and took a beer. The chip stand was two houses away from where Malinda's oldest sister, Olive, lived.

She said to Brian, "Let me out, I want to go to the bathroom at my sister's house." Brian opened the door and got out of the car.

Malinda left and stayed the remainder of the weekend with her sister. She went to school from there on Monday morning.

At school, Janie asked Malinda, "Why did you leave? Brian likes you a lot. Do you like him?" Malinda answered indifferently, "Yeah."

The following Sunday, JJ and Brian picked up Malinda in the middle of the afternoon and brought her back home at three o'clock in the morning. She expected her parents to question her whereabouts, but they did and said nothing. Malinda thought, N*ext time, I'll stay out all night. For sure they'll react then.* On Friday Janie made plans to get together with Brian and Paul. She said to Malinda, "Did you know Brian bought a car and he's picking you up on Saturday? There's going to be a party at his house." Malinda went to Janie's house after school. As planned, Brian picked up Malinda and drove to his house, which was in the country on a dairy farm. The house was a large bungalow that was fairly new. There was a barn in the yard and a shed. Brian held Malinda's hand and walked her to the house. When they entered, a teenage girl was on her way downstairs carrying a basin of dirty dishes. She said, "Let me by."

Brian said, "That's my sister." They went up a couple of steps to the kitchen where Brian's mother introduced herself and told them to keep their boots on or they would get slivers in their feet. The floors were of plywood and worn out in the heavier traffic areas. The walls were covered with exposed gyp rock that was never painted. There were more dirty dishes piled up on a homemade countertop with clean dishes underneath it. There were no kitchen cupboards. Brian led Malinda past the kitchen and into the living room. He went to an armchair where his father was sitting and said, "This is Pops. My friends call him Hero. He knows commando fighting from the army – Five years in the front lines. Anybody who fights him loses."

His father said, "Hello, sit down. I'm going to make some tea. Do you want some?" Brian and Malinda sat on the couch. When his father stood up, his six-foot build was firm and muscular. Brian said, "Try punching him in the stomach." Malinda answered, "No, I don't want to do that."

When his father came back into the room, Brian got up and walked toward his dad. He took the cup of hot tea from his father's hand and placed it on a coffee table. Then with closed fists, he positioned himself and said, "Come on, Pops, let's see what you got."

His father let Brian punch him as hard as he could, but the large man did not flinch. Then with one arm, he gently threw his son to the floor.

Brian said," I let him win because he's an old man." His father sat down in his easy chair and asked if they wanted to watch the news and the weather. He said, "I never miss this sweetheart anchor woman."

Brian's mother was in the kitchen making apple pies. When they were in the oven baking, she joined them in the living room with her cup of tea and sat next to Brian. Malinda asked where the bathroom was. "It's downstairs," Brian answered. Malinda left the room and went downstairs. Brian's sister was at the laundry tubs washing dishes. There was no sink in the kitchen.

Malinda asked, "Where's the bathroom?" The sister pointed to a curtain and said, "Right behind there." The toilet seat was a homemade wooden platform with a pail underneath. When Malinda walked out, Brian's sister said, "There's a shower in the milk house, you know."

There was a full set of drums in the living room. Malinda asked, "Whose are those?" Brian answered, "My brother's." A few moments later, two carloads of teens arrived. Janie and Paul entered the house with JJ followed by a dozen or so other teens. Most of them were school dropouts. Some of them were from Malinda's class who were known as troublemakers. Others were strangers from the city. The bunch brought with them several cases of beer, which they piled high on the living room floor.

JJ said, "Let's crack open these babies." He took a beer and said, "The first one's for Hero." Brian's dad took the beer and thanked JJ. Brian's older brother and girlfriend entered the room carrying an elaborate stereo system.

"That's my brother, Thomas," said Brian. Thomas set up his sound system and put on loud music sung by "Led Zeppelan." Brian went to the drums and played them loudly. The teens drank beer, smoked cigarettes and talked at the top of their lungs. Malinda was impressed by Brian's drumming. Brian's parents were cheerful and welcomed all the visitors.

About an hour later, an older couple walked in. The man had a bottle of whiskey in his hand. Brian said to Malinda, "That's my favourite auntie and uncle." Brian's parents went with the couple into the kitchen to play cards.

The party moved to the basement. Brian and his friends smoked pot. Some were doing acid. Paul asked Malinda if she wanted some. She said, "Thanks, no." In order not to draw further attention, she accepted a bottle of beer when it was offered to her. No one noticed that she held the same bottle all evening. Brian stayed close to Malinda and guarded her like a prized possession.

The party ended around 2 a.m. Janie met Malinda at the doorway and said, "You should stay here tonight. I'm going with Paul." Brian said to Malinda, "You could, you know." Malinda responded, "But what about your parents?" Brian replied, "Ah, they're cool." After everyone left Brian took Malinda by the hand and showed her to the double bed in a far corner of the basement. He said, "Sit down. I'll get you some blankets." Malinda sat on the edge of the bed. When Brian returned, he said, "Here, lie down. You must be tired." "Yeah, I am," answered Malinda. Then Brian placed his hands on her shoulders and gently laid her back. He tucked a blanket around her and said, "Can I hold you until you fall asleep?" Malinda nodded and closed her eyes. Brian lay beside her, wrapped her in his arms and she fell asleep.

During the night she was awakened by Brian's kisses. When she opened her eyes he said, "I love you," then lightly stroked her breasts. Malinda remained still. After more petting and kissing, Brian positioned himself under the blanket and lay on top of her. He was naked and Malinda could feel his erect penis rubbing against her body. She wanted to stop him but she froze. Brian unbuttoned Malinda's shirt and continued to kiss her. He gently pushed one sleeve down and then the other. He felt his way to the clasps of her bra and unhooked them. He removed her bra. He kissed her breasts then sucked on one of her nipples as he unbuttoned her jeans and pulled down the zipper. He placed one hand on her vagina and with the other pulled down her jeans along with her panties. With his penis, he penetrated her. Right after they had sex, Brian fell asleep. That night, she lay awake thinking, *the words, I love you, are very special words only to be used when one really means it*. That night she heard those words for the first time. She concluded, *he must really love me*.

The next day around noon, Malinda heard JJ come in the door and say, "Where's Brian." Then she heard him come down the stairs. He was loud and shouted, "Come on you lazy asses, get up!" He sat on the bed and offered Brian a beer. The two friends drank and Malinda was embarrassed to be seen lying in bed with Brian. Then JJ and Brian went upstairs leaving Malinda to get dressed.

She found them with Brian's parents in the kitchen. His father was having a beer with the boys and his mother was cooking. She greeted Malinda and said, "You guys are staying for dinner. I'm making roast chicken and a peach pie." Malinda spent the day with Brian and stayed overnight again. On Monday morning, she joined Brian's sister on her school bus. Malinda was in a daze all day at school thinking about Brian's affectionate lovemaking. After school she went with Lorraine on her usual bus route home.

The fear of receiving a beating at home diminished but the belief that she was unwanted at home grew. When Malinda arrived home, there was a pot of soup simmering on the stove. Her mother did not mention anything about Malinda's two-day absence and later, neither did her father. Malinda cried herself to sleep that night and thought, *Lorraine's parents would frantically look for her if she didn't come home one night. I was gone for two nights and they didn't even phone Brian's house to find out if I was alright. They don't want me.*

Brian threatened other males that wanted to be with her. He did not attend the next high school dance. Malinda took a ride home with Lorraine's brother. The following week, Malinda heard that Brian went to Ste. Agnes and beat him up. When Malinda asked Brian why he did that, he answered, "Because I love you so much; it makes me crazy." His words had the power to make her feel special and she overlooked his jealousy and possessiveness. During the course of time, she also ignored his heavy use of alcohol and drugs. Outings with his friends included breaking the law and fighting against other gangs. Malinda minimized the seriousness of his criminal activities.

Brian and Paul were charged with several counts of breaking and entering with theft over five thousand dollars. They were caught with stolen boat motors, miscellaneous auto parts and tools. Brian spent a brief time in juvenile jail. He phoned Malinda from the shut-in. Malinda announced that she did not want to see him any more, but Brian pleaded, saying that he needed her in order to stay out of trouble. At the same time, she could hear the echoes of religious teachings that stated having sex without being married to the person was a serious sin. To avoid being condemned, she made a bargain with God that if she was with only Brian, it would nullify her offense.

As soon as Brian was released from jail he went to see Malinda. They sat in his car and talked. Brian said that he had learned his lesson and promised Malinda repeatedly that he would change. To prove himself trustworthy, he asserted, "This car is mine and it's all legal and everything. I'm going to get a job. Maddy, I'm changing, but I need you to keep me out of trouble." Malinda believed that he was sincere. Her brother, Hubert, owned a small contracting business and she asked him to hire Brian. The job required that Brian own a truck and tools. Brian was able to borrow money for the equipment and started to work. Later in the year, Malinda moved out of her parents' home to live in Youville with her older sister, Olive. She spent every weekend at Brian's place.

When Malinda completed grade eleven, she moved to another older brother's house in the city to attend a one-year course at a community college. A few weeks later, Brian arranged for a neighbour who worked in the city to drive Malinda to college each day. This way, he would have someone keep close tabs on her whereabouts. "I can't be away from you," he told her. Brian convinced her to move in with him and his parents. At Christmas, Brian surprised her with an engagement ring. Malinda set the wedding date for after her graduation in July.

Although Malinda's father had paid for all his oldest daughters' weddings, he refused to pay for this one. The news was bittersweet as Malinda wanted to have a small wedding anyway; however, Brian's mother insisted that all her relatives be invited. "In our family we always invite everybody to a wedding," she implored. "I'm working. The bank will lend me the money to pay for the wedding." She met with Malinda's father and convinced him to pay for the hall. He said, "But, I'm not paying for the alcohol."

Brian's mother said, "If you pay for the hall, we'll pay for the meal and alcohol." Brian's mother hired a photographer. She ordered alcohol and hired a caterer to make the wedding cake and meals for two hundred people. Malinda borrowed a wedding dress that Hubert's wife wore for their wedding. Brian's mother sewed the dresses for two bridesmaids and a flower girl. Tom would be in charge of the bar. Two weeks before the wedding, Tom and his wife held a social evening for Brian and Malinda.

During the wedding reception, some of Malinda's older siblings and in-laws confronted Tom and accused him of stealing money and alcohol from the social evening. Tom denied the accusation. He told them he did not want to get in an argument on his brother's wedding night. When the wedding was over, Tom and Brian's friends packed up what was left of the alcohol and cases of empty beer bottles. After the guests left, Malinda's older siblings confronted Tom outside. Her sister, Georgette, said, "Did you count the full boxes of beer and bottles of whisky? If you don't return those to the liquor commission, you'll have to pay for them." Another asked, "Where are you taking this booze?"

Tom replied, "I'm taking it to my parents' house where the after party is." Georgette followed Tom and when he collected the cash and envelopes of money that had been presented by the guests, she taunted him, saying, "Make sure you give Brian and Malinda that money." Brian's friends got involved. A fight erupted between the men but ended quickly. Before they left, Georgette shouted, "We're not going to your wild party. We're having a decent one at my parents' and we don't want you there."

Malinda was unaware of the friction between the two families until later at the after party. The men got crazy drunk and talked about the argument. They got all worked up and decided to finish the fight at Malinda's parents' home where her family was partying. Brian and his friends left to round up some tire bars and pieces of towing-chains. Brian got in his truck along with two of his friends. Tom and the other friends crammed together in three more vehicles. Malinda ran to Brian's truck and opened the driver's door. She stood outside and pleaded with him not to do this. Brian told her to back up and close the door. When she did, he raced away. His spinning tires threw gravel from the driveway and a large stone hit Malinda on her hip. She was left by herself injured and in a cloud of dust. When she re-entered the house, she found that Brian's parents had gone to bed. Malinda retreated in the basement to the bed where she and Brian had made love for the first time. She lay in a foetal position and anesthetised from feeling her physical and emotional pain.

A couple of hours later, Malinda heard footsteps coming down the basement stairs. Then she heard her brother Adelard's voice say, "Where's the light switch?" The lights turned on. Adelard walked over to the bed where Malinda lay and stood there. He had Brian by the hand with him. He took Malinda's hand and Malinda grasped it with all her strength. Adelard looked at Brian and said, "Your place tonight is with her." Somehow he had managed to appease Brian. He led the young groom and his new bride up the staircase while Brian's friends followed and shouted threats at him. On the porch outside, one of them kicked him from behind, but Adelard ignored the provocation and walked to Brian's truck. He opened the door and told Malinda to get in first, and then Brian sat in the driver's seat. Adelard closed the door and said, "Now, go home." Adelard got in his truck and drove away. No one went after him. The newlyweds drove straight to the city where they rented a cheap apartment to be their new marital home. Malinda said nothing to Brian about his behavior.

The next day Malinda was making breakfast when Brian's friends dropped by. Brian sat with them in the living room and Malinda stayed in the kitchen. She overheard them talking about the feud of the night before and was relieved to learn that no one got hurt and that the weapons were never used. However, she was greatly ashamed that her husband had humiliated and dishonoured her family. After the friends left, Malinda said to Brian, "We should go to my dad and apologize for troubling him."

Brian got upset and said, "Your place is now with your husband; not your father." At that moment, another teaching echoed that a wife's place was with her husband. Malinda's rationale was cut short and visits with her family halted.

Malinda got a desk job at an insurance company. Christmas was a few days away and she wondered if they should go to her family's annual "reveillon", the gathering after midnight mass. She said to Brian, "No one in my family has ever missed the Christmas Eve celebrations. We should go." He refused and said, "We're going to my parents' place and we're staying there."

On Christmas Eve, Brian said, "If you want to go - go, but I'm staying right here." Although Malinda dreaded facing her family, she did not want to be the first in the family to break with family tradition at Christmas. Malinda went to midnight mass in her hometown, after which she drove to her parents' place. Along the way, she resolved that if she were challenged about the trouble on her wedding night, she would not take part in a quarrel and would peaceably leave.

Malinda entered her parents' house. It was noisy. The yearly gathering became large since the older siblings married and had children of their own. The adult men drank whiskey and beer. Malinda's father did his traditional rounds of homebrew, offering a one-ounce shot glass to each family member sixteen years of age and older. Malinda's mother set up a small table for seven little children, then she returned to her stove and made coffee. The aroma of roast turkey filled the kitchen as she opened the oven door and removed the lid from the pan with the roasted bird inside. The end of the sound of the electric knife signalled that the turkey was carved. After she mashed the potatoes, Malinda's mother called the little children to sit at a little table just for kids. Then, she put all the hot dishes of food on the main table and the family feasted. The children were noisy and excited. They ate quickly and resumed their play with their new toys. The adults chatted about their work and cracked a few jokes. All of a sudden, things turned sour for Malinda. Georgette turned to her father and said, "I can't believe how our family was disgraced by Brian and his gang of hooligans who came here to fight us." Malinda said nothing and hoped no one else would.

Then her father nodded his agreement and, just as though Malinda was not there, he said, "This has never happened to this family ever before. Why, they came here with chains to fight!" Malinda kept quiet. To hide from the conversation she bowed her head toward the table. She could not ignore her father's distressed tone. She got up from the table and pretended she had to go to the bathroom. Once there, she reassured herself that she could muster up enough courage to walk past them and leave. She heard a tap on the door and her sister, Olive said, "It's me, Olive." Malinda did not answer. Again, Olive spoke, "Come on out and join us. Georgette is just trying to make trouble." Malinda answered, "I don't want trouble on Christmas." Olive rebutted, "Don't pay attention to what she said and just ignore her. It's early morning and dad had too much to drink."

Malinda did not respond and after a moment Olive went away. When Malinda came out, she passed by her parents' bedroom. The door was open and she saw her father sitting on the edge of his bed with a clean pair of coveralls on. He reached for a pair of wool socks and was about to put one on when Malinda entered the room. It was 5 a.m. and milking time. She wanted to tell him good-bye and apologize for offending him on her wedding night but when she stood close to him, she suddenly wrapped her arms around his head and kissed him on his bald spot. What came next was not an apology, but she did something unexpected and said, "I love you, dad." Malinda released her hold and her father looked toward the floor uttering, "J'ai jamais voulu te faire mal. (I never wanted to hurt you)." Malinda was a little perplexed by his reaction. She could not figure out why *he* would apologize.

Malinda caught Brian twice with other women and she left him. Brian quit his job with Hubert. After they were apart for ten months, Malinda forgave his unfaithfulness. The hope of salvaging the marriage rested on her husband's need for her. She spent most of the earnings from her job on his lawyers. He often turned his rage toward her and threatened her with knives. Sometimes he would beat her. Still Malinda stayed with him strengthened by those rare occasions when he would make her feel special. After every violent episode, a recognizable cycle would repeat itself. Brian used the sad puppy look to lure Malinda into feeling sorry for him. Time and again, she fell for the tactic of his apologies and promises about how he was going to change. When she forgave him, he was pleasant for a while. He would be on his best behavior, but then a tension would build. Soon blame, put downs, anger and drunkenness would follow in a predictable pattern. Malinda did not want anyone to know how he treated her. She felt that if anyone found out, she would be ridiculed for being stupid enough to marry someone who beat her. No one knew. Malinda thought about leaving him again, but she did not want to be the first in her family to divorce. That would only re-affirm to her father that he was right about her. Failing at marriage was not something Malinda wanted him to add to his list of her no good for nothing deeds. Unrealistic optimism and false hopes kept her stuck in a dangerous marriage. Malinda reminded herself that her upbringing taught her that marriage was difficult and that everyone had a cross to bear.

Malinda believed she could help Brian become the person he claimed he could be. This time she recommended him to Olive's husband for work. For some time it looked like things would change. Malinda stopped taking birth control pills and became pregnant. Brian got into a fight at work and quit his job. His alcoholism got progressively worse. So did Malinda's state of mind. The more she believed he would change, the more his actions mirrored the opposite. His jealousy and violence went from bad to worst. He succeeded in isolating her from her family and all her friends.

Four Dead in Car Crash

Malinda was five months pregnant when they were awakened in the early morning by their telephone ringing. Brian got up to answer the call. Malinda could tell there was bad news at the other end of the line. Brian only repeated his preferred four-letter "F" word. She got up to stand by her husband. As soon as he hung up, she asked, "What is it?"

He replied bluntly, "It's your parents; they're dead! They're all dead: your parents, Adelard and his wife too. They had a car accident. They're all dead!"

Malinda felt she should say something or cry. Neither words nor tears came. Suddenly she felt sharp stomach cramps and quickly ran to the bathroom. She felt guilty that she developed diarrhoea rather than tears.

News about the accident and pictures of her four dead family members appeared in newspapers across Canada. The tragedy made the news on television and radio stations with the headline, "Five killed in car crash." The driver of the colliding vehicle also died.

An unprecedented funeral was held in Youville. On the way to the funeral with Brian, Malinda heard the song, "Chariots of Fire", on the car radio. When she entered the church she saw four coffins. The caskets were closed. The funeral director said the bodies were dismembered and beyond recognition. A picture of each of the deceased was centered on top of each casket. The coffins of her mother and father were alongside each other and those of Adelard and his wife rested behind them.

Malinda and Brian sat at the front of the church with the rest of her family. The mass began. Georgette offered her siblings each an anti-anxiety pill from a labelled bottle of medication, which she got from her doctor. She said, "Here, this will keep you from crying."

Malinda said, "No thanks. I don't need it." She was numb and could not grieve. She turned and saw behind them the pack of people sitting tightly against each other in the pews. Others stood wherever they could. The vestibule was packed with people who did not arrive early enough to get seats.

Malinda noticed Adelard's four children with his relatives. Amidst hundreds of people, they appeared so totally alone. Adelard's eldest was eleven and his youngest child was two. Malinda realized that their lifelines had been taken from them. She thought *My nieces and nephew are orphaned! How can this horrible thing happen to them?* When she saw the tears on their faces, Malinda became overwhelmed with tears of her own.

The families of the deceased parents faced a mountain of problems. It was difficult to sort out which one to undertake first. There were children to find homes for and a large farm to run. Adelard lived in a town nearby and operated an auto repair shop. His children were staying with his mother-in-law until suitable caregivers were appointed. Someone would have to shut down his business. The executor of the estate of Malinda's father met with the family for a reading of the Will. He said, "The girls are not going to like what's in it." He opened the meeting and said, "Your mother had no Will; therefore, her estate is divided equally among her children. You will need to appoint an executor for her estate. Adelard had no Will so his entire estate is divided equally among his children. He had a good life insurance policy. Executors for his and his wife's estate will also need to be appointed." He took a sip of his coffee and opened an envelope that contained the Will. He continued, "Your father had a Will in which he gives one third of his estate to your mother. The remaining two-thirds are to be divided equally among his sons. To his daughters, he leaves three hundred dollars each."

Olive said, "But our father had no debts, and his three houses and lands must be worth close to two hundred thousand dollars. I am the eldest of this family and worked on this farm just as hard as my brothers did."

That night, Olive was appointed executrix for her mother's estate. A few weeks passed, and then Olive called a meeting with her siblings. Those who were married came with their spouses. Olive opened the meeting and said, "The girls equally contributed to the success of this family. Adelard had asthma and because of his allergies, I had to work with dad. Mom and dad did not have any more children until six years after Adelard was born. I worked hard on this farm." Olive's husband came to his wife's defence, and said, "Each one of you helped on the farm. While Georgette cooked and cleaned inside the house, the rest of you milked cows and helped your father."

The older boys were quiet. Georgette said, "The girls should get an equal share of the estate."

Hubert's wife said, "Your father made a Will for a reason. He wanted his sons to inherit the farm."

Georgette rebutted, "That Will was made twenty-three years ago just before they moved to this farm. Since then, things changed drastically. Dad inherited his father's house and also bought a rental house in town." Hubert and his closest brother defended their position in the Will.

Then Malinda asked, "Isn't a Will etched in stone and cannot be changed?"

Olive answered, "I hired a lawyer for mom's estate and he said that certainly we can oppose the Will. We'll have to sue and contest it." The older siblings and their spouses began to argue. While the feud was going on, Malinda tuned out the hostility and thought, *even after he is dead, dad manages to give me one last slap in the face.* She knew all too well that he viewed women to be less worthy.

Brian whispered to Malinda, "This is none of my business. It's between you and your family members. I'm going home. Are you coming?" Malinda left with her husband.

The death of her parents left Malinda with many regrets. Her unborn child would never get to know the grandmother who made little breads for her grandchildren. She thought about the times when her mother would play the violin and watched the grandchildren dance and that, every Sunday, the grandchildren visited Grandma and Grandpa on the farm. But mostly, Malinda regretted that it was too late to repair the unsettling relationship between her and her father.

Brian's father told Malinda that if she had a boy, he would give her five hundred dollars. Four months later, Nadine was born. Malinda had no visitors come to see her and the baby in the hospital. After a three-day drunk, Brian came to see his new family at the hospital. His clothes were dirty and smelly. Malinda and the baby were to go home the next day. Brian got his truck stuck on the riverbank past the hospital parkade. The three of them had to take a taxi home.

Nadine had dark brown eyes and curly hair that became bronzed by the sun in the summertime. Malinda cherished every moment with her little girl. When her maternity leave elapsed, she went back to her work. She got along well with her co-workers. They were the only friends she had. During coffee break one day, the group talked about weight gain. Malinda engaged in the usual chatter and said that she had ten pounds to shed from the aftermath of her pregnancy. One of them commented that smoking cigarettes cuts the appetite and if you smoke only five or six a day, the doctors say that it would not damage your lungs. A few days later, Malinda decided to smoke and bought a package of menthol cigarettes. During coffee break the next day, Malinda joined her counterparts and lit a cigarette. "I'll keep it down to six a day," she stated. In three weeks, Malinda lost the pounds but she continued to smoke.

Brian's insecurities increased. One Saturday evening there was a staff dinner and dance that it was important to attend. Brian knew of the upcoming event. Malinda was getting dressed and told Brian he should get ready. Instead, he walked to the fridge and got himself a beer. Malinda shouted from the bedroom, "I got your clothes ready." When there was no answer, Malinda went to the kitchen and repeated her message. Brian was sitting at the kitchen table and said, "We should take Nadine and go to my parents' place for the rest of the weekend. We'll go riding on my brother's snow machine."

Malinda remained calm and said, "Nadine is already at the sitters next door. It's important for us to go tonight." Brian's jaw started to quiver, a reaction that Malinda knew occurred just before he blew up. She tried to persuade him and said, "Come on, Brian, we'll leave shortly after supper and we can go to your parents' first thing in the morning."

Brian lit a cigarette and declared, "I'm not going there. We're going to my parents'."

Malinda stood her ground and said, "Then I'll phone Mona from work. She lives nearby and she'll pick me up."

Brian guzzled his last drops of beer and slammed the empty bottle on the kitchen table. He walked over to the fridge and got another. He stood there and waited while Malinda finished her conversation and hung up the phone. Then he rushed toward her and knocked her down to the floor. He sat on her stomach and commanded, "You're not going anywhere!" He put both his hands around her throat and shouted, "You want to go slutting around, don't you?" Malinda struggled to get loose. Just then, Mona arrived and knocked on the door. No one answered so she let herself in and shouted, "Hello-o! It's me, Mona." Brian immediately released his grip and stood up. Mona walked in and saw Malinda still on the floor. She had a puzzled look on her face and asked, "What are you doing on the floor?"

Malinda got up and answered, "He was choking me." Then Malinda looked at Brian, but he was sitting quietly at the kitchen table. For the first time Malinda decided to tell someone and also call the police. She went to the phonebook and dialled the number. An enforcement officer answered the call and stated his name. Malinda said, "My husband had me on the floor and was choking me." The officer's sneering comment was, "Well, he's not choking you now, is he." Malinda hung up the phone. Mona just stood there. Brian remained quiet. Malinda and her friend left.

When Malinda returned, Brian and the baby were gone, but returned the following night without more conflict. Calling the police for help was not something Malinda ever wanted to consider again.

After that night, a few years went by without any violence erupting between Brian and Malinda. Brian got a job in a factory and gave his pay checks to Malinda to look after the household bills. Between the two incomes, Malinda put away one hundred dollars a month for a down payment on a house. Brian still drank a lot but did not get violent. Malinda thought he was cured from raging anger. She planned to have another baby, but the apartment was already too small for Nadine to grow up in. After three years, the savings totalled three thousand dollars. When Brian's mother heard of their plans to buy a house, she said to them, "We are giving you a five-acre parcel of land anywhere you'd like on our farmland. It will cost a lot less money to have a brand new bungalow built here rather than buy an old house in the city.

Tom could find a good used car for Malinda to go to work in," she continued. Malinda told Brian that she liked living in the city.

"We're both close to our work. We won't have to pay so much for fuel." But the real reason was that she wanted to continue her marriage at a distance from her meddling mother-in-law. Brian accepted the parcel of land without Malinda's say and asserted, "I'm only signing papers for a house if we move it onto our lot." Malinda settled for the idea with the understanding that their lot be located at the farthest north-eastern corner of the farm.

Malinda, Brian and his mother went to see a builder in the area and came home at the end of the day having ordered a ready-to-move house. Malinda got to pick the style of kitchen cabinets, light fixtures and flooring pattern from a few selections. To save money they decided to paint the interior themselves. Some work costs went over budget for the well, sewage system and the installation of a new driveway and culvert. After the move, Malinda's brothers and sisters began to accept Brian in the family. When he drank he was comical and made them laugh. Her brothers invited him to play drums when they jammed together and when they had a gig.

Money was tight. The mortgage payment and commuting to the city on a daily basis ate up almost all their income. The heating costs rose in the winter. Brian got an old wood burning barrel stove from a co-worker who was going to throw it out. On the weekends he and his father drove to the nearest provincial forestry-logging site. They brought home wood slabs that the cutting crew let them have for free. Sometimes Malinda left Nadine with her mother-in-law to go with them. Malinda packed wieners and marshmallows to roast on a fire and the men brought whiskey *to warm their bones while they picked wood*, they joked. That forest was more gigantic than the one of her childhood. It was a pine forest and it had a river that flowed through it. In the summer they went fishing there. When the mother-in-law came along, Malinda brought Nadine and the family enjoyed the day together fishing and picnicking. Before the ride back home, Brian drove along the logging trails to identify where the game was for when hunting season opened. But, for the moment, Malinda got to spot deer and partridge amidst this gigantic wilderness. Brian's father talked about his ancestors, the voyageurs, and how they hunted for beaver, fox and wolf. They would walk and portage all the way to the city where they sold their pelts to the northwest fur trade company. He also explained how he was related to some famous warriors and he spoke about their Métis heritage. It was Malinda's favorite outing to venture into the woodlands and to listen to the stories.

Two years went by and Malinda wanted another baby. She got pregnant and Brian asked for a lay off at work. He talked about joining some of his friends where they worked in another province. "There are plenty of home renovation contracts because of a recent hailstorm," he said. Malinda did not like the idea because those friends were his old drinking buddies. "Our baby will be born soon," Malinda said as though Brian needed to be reminded of that fact. Brian said, "It's only temporary. I have a chance to make a lot of money." Malinda saw that he was determined and knew he would not change his mind. She asked, "Will you hitch a ride with them or take the truck?"

Brian answered, "I'll need the truck for work." "Then," Malinda replied, "I won't be able to get wood." Brian reassured her, "I'll make three times the money. We could afford the heat bill and I'll get the neighbour to do the snow clearing in the yard."

His friends were back in town. For the next few days, Brian spent a lot of time with them and came home drunk. Malinda was in her bedroom getting ready for bed one night when Brian came in and shouted, "Anybody in this fucking house?"

Malinda answered in a quivering voice, "I'm in here, in the bedroom." She heard heavy footsteps from Brian's boots stomping down the hallway. She was naked and about to put on her nightgown when Brian came in the room and pushed her. Malinda fell backwards on the bed. Brian leaped beside her and raised a closed fist to her face. He reeked of alcohol. Just before he hit her, Malinda had no fear and looked at her seven-month pregnant belly. Then, she looked at her husband straight in the eyes and said, "I had a small flame of love left for you, but you just put it out." She boldly stared him in the face, expecting to be punched but Brian unclenched his fist and left. Malinda got up and checked on Nadine then she went to bed. She woke up the next day with the conviction that she had no more love left for her husband and that, henceforth, she would devote all her love to her babies.

Before Brian left to work out of the province, Malinda told him that she planned to take Nadine and leave him. Brian alleged that no man was going to want her with two kids, especially a newborn, and that she would end up on the welfare roll. She believed his statement to be true. It was a frightening thought to have to leave and support herself and two young children, one of them would be a newborn baby.

Brian was working on his truck to get it ready for the long trip across the province. Malinda waited until she had his full attention and said, "I wont' leave but from now on, we will live separate lives. I will live my life the way I want to and you live yours the way you want to." Brian ignored her statement and continued to get ready. He packed a suitcase with clothes and set it by the door with the rest of his gear. Before he walked out the door he said, "I'm leaving now." Malinda did not acknowledge him. He came in and out several times while loading his gear. On the last haul, he said, "I'll mail you my pay check." He wanted a good-bye kiss but Malinda refused to give him one. She said, "I don't care what you do." Brian whispered, "Good-bye."

A couple of months later Malinda went on maternity leave. She received a check from Brian and paid off the overdue electricity and telephone bills. There was not enough money to bring the mortgage up to date. A few weeks later, she went into labour and gave birth to another beautiful little girl. This one had blond hair and blue eyes. She named her Suzanne. Brian showed up at the hospital looking and smelling like he had not bathed in weeks. He kissed Malinda on the cheek and said, "My mother called to tell me you were in labour and that the neighbour is keeping Nadine and her husband drove you to the hospital. I left right away but I can't stay. I've been driving for fourteen hours straight and I'm starving. Mother said she had a hot meal waiting for me."

Malinda held her new baby snugly against her breast and said, "She's beautiful and cuddly." Brian lifted Malinda's left hand and noticed that Malinda had no wedding ring on. On his way out he grumbled, "She's not a boy."

When Malinda returned home, Brian stayed for three weeks then announced that he was leaving again for work out of town, "I probably won't be back before Christmas." Malinda had an announcement of her own.

She said, "We're no longer married. Only because I can't leave with a newborn baby and a toddler am I living in the same house with you." Brian ignored his wife's comment as she continued to say, "You live your life the way you want to and I'll live mine the way I want to."

After Brian left, Malinda babysat other children and used her maternity leave benefits to buy food and pay the utility bills. One Friday afternoon Malinda babysat Tom's two children while he and his wife went to the city. When they returned, Tom phoned from his mother's house and asked Malinda to bring his children there, that his mother was making dinner for everyone. When she arrived, Tom's friend, Eric, was there. Eric lived in the city and worked with inner city kids as a youth counsellor. He was single and Malinda found him attractive.

After dinner Malinda went home and put her children to bed. Shortly after, Tom and Eric dropped in for a visit. Malinda was aware that Tom and his wife had an open marriage that allowed each to have other sexual partners. Tom often admitted to Malinda how he wanted to have sex with as many women as he possibly could. It was unusual for Tom to come over. He usually stayed around his or his parents' house a mile down the road. Malinda was not comfortable with his visit. Tom had a six-pack of beer and said he wanted to sit in the living room. He and Eric took a beer. When they offered one to Malinda, she politely turned it down. "No thanks, I have to get up early," she said. The three carried on some light conversation when Tom suggested that Malinda sleep with both of them. Malinda pretended not to hear his proposition. Tom stepped out to use the washroom. Malinda was alone with Eric and said, "I want you to stay, but I want Tom to go."

When Tom returned, Eric got up and led him to the kitchen to have a private chat. Malinda heard the door open and close. Eric came back to the living room and said, "He's gone." Eric lit the candle on the coffee table and sat on the floor. He said, "Come Malinda, join me here, it's much more comfortable than the couch." The atmosphere was relaxing. Eric talked about his life in the city and how he came out to the country to get some needed 'R&R'. Malinda was quiet and just listened. Eric said he wanted to look into her eyes. He reached for her hand and gently pulled her to face him. Then he kissed her passionately. She felt tingling everywhere in her body. After a while, Malinda took Eric by the hand and helped him up. Eric followed her to the bedroom.

He stayed for the entire night. Malinda experienced an orgasm for the first time.

In the morning Malinda got up before the children did and Eric followed suit. He had a shower while Malinda made him breakfast. When Eric entered the kitchen he greeted Malinda with a caress and gently kissed her. She ran her fingers through his wet locks of black hair, then she gazed into his sparkling dark eyes and said, "You look and smell really nice." Then the children woke up and Malinda dressed and fed them. Eric and Malinda had their breakfast. When the children were done Malinda encouraged them to play in the living room. She returned to the kitchen and lit a cigarette. She and Eric chatted over a cup of coffee. Eric looked at Malinda from across the table and said, "You are an amazing woman." Malinda didn't know how to take his compliment about her. It boost up her self-confidence that she could attract a gentle man with an intellectual background.

The next time Brian phoned, Malinda told him that their house had to be put up for sale. "The bank sent a letter. They want the arrears paid up by the end of this month. We have no choice," she said. Malinda hired a real estate agent. Three weeks later an offer was made on the house. Malinda signed the documents. When the agent phoned Brian to fax him the copy to sign, Brian said he would rather take the next flight home and sign the papers the next day. That evening Brian phoned Malinda. He spoke with a soft voice and said, "I'm at the airport." Malinda asked, "Who's picking you up?" Brian answered, "I called Tom and he can't come but he'll lend you his truck for you to pick me up." Malinda sighed and said, "I can't do that. The girls are in bed." He responded, "Tom is bringing my mom over to baby-sit and I'll wait for you." Malinda protested, "It's going to take at least a couple of hours for me to get there." Brian replied, "I'll wait for you." Malinda was about to say good-bye when Brian whispered, "Malinda, I want to come back to stay." Malinda said nothing. Then Brian continued, "The girls need a daddy." "It's too late," she said. "The house is sold. There's a little bit of profit from the sale. We'll split it and I'm going to move back to the city with the girls." To Brian's promise that he was changed for good, Malinda rebutted, "I've heard that before and it didn't happen. I don't believe you any more."

"Malinda, I'm not drinking any more," Brian declared. "I want my family. We'll all move together to the city. I'm different now! You'll see that if you just let me prove it to you!" Malinda said, "Tom is here. I'll be there as soon as I can."

During the drive to the airport, Malinda thought, *what if he really is changed? I might be leaving him just when he is finally sincere and he is changed. I couldn't bear it if we divorced and he remained a good man but found someone else to have a good marriage with.* Malinda thought hard about what to do. In the end she went with the dream of finally having a loving husband. Her conscience began to bother her about Eric and she thought, *if we are going to start with a clean slate, I will have to be completely honest.*

After Brian signed the papers, they ventured into the city and bought a tiny old house that needed a lot of repairs. The move was scheduled for one month from then. Brian and Malinda were happy and Malinda recognized change in Brian. He was sober and fun to be with. With the help of a neighbor, he built a large wooden dollhouse for Nadine. Malinda painted and decorated it.

One evening he had his hand on the door handle with his coat on when little Nadine went to him and tugged at his coat. She looked up with her big brown eyes and repeatedly said, "*Toto*," which in French baby talk meant car. Nadine wanted to go with her father for a car ride. Malinda asked Brian where he was going. He answered, "I'm just going with my pop to hunt gophers in his field. Brian ignored the little girl so Malinda asked, "Why don't you take her with you?" On his way out Brian answered, "Cus she's not a boy."

A week later, Brian and Malinda drove past their little house in the city. Brian said, "I'm going to buy a fishing boat and we'll all go fishing." Malinda looked at the yard and planned where a sand box and swings for the kids would go. She exclaimed, "Oh, look, Brian, that would be a great spot to plant some of my favourite flowers and a garden!"

They went out for dinner. During the meal, Malinda said, "Brian, there's something I want to tell you. It's about when you were away and we were separated."

Curious, Brian asked, "What is it?"

Malinda proceeded, "You know how I forgave you when you cheated on me more than once?" Brian didn't answer, just kept listening. Malinda continued, "Well, when I told you we were separated, a short time after that I too slept with someone." Brian asked, "Who?" Malinda hesitated, then said, "I am only telling you because our new life together should begin with a clean slate." Brian questioned, "Was it with my brother? Because if it was, then that's okay." Malinda answered, "No, it was with his friend, Eric."

That night when they got home, Malinda put the girls to bed. Brian left for a couple of hours. When he returned, Brian raged against Malinda and charged that Suzanne was not his child. He stomped his way to the bedroom. Malinda followed him to try and reason with him. Brian was in front of the closet and reached for his shotgun. He snapped the weapon open and loaded it. Malinda turned pale with fright and felt a cold sensation. With a shaking voice, she blurted out, "Brian, don't fuck around with guns!" He turned toward Malinda and raised the gun. Malinda looked into both barrels of the loaded shot gun which pointed at her face.

"Get the fuck out of here!" he shouted. Immediately Malinda ran out of the house. She got in the truck and hoped that the keys were in it. She kept her head low and saw the keys in the ignition. She hastily drove without the lights on for fear that he would fire at the vehicle. She drove to Tom's place and ran inside his house. "I have to use the phone!" she exclaimed. Tom and his wife saw that she was barefoot. Malinda dialled Olive's house and her husband answered. "Brian has a gun in the house and he's alone with Nadine and Suzanne. Go and talk to him. He'll listen to you." Olive's husband answered, "He has a loaded gun?" Malinda was frantic. "Yeah, and I'm scared he might shoot the kids!" Her brother-in-law instructed, "Call the cops."

"But that will make him more mad! It's better if you go!" shouted Malinda.

"He's got a loaded gun and I'm not going to mess with that!" said the brother-in-law. Malinda hung up the phone and turned to Tom and begged *him* to go.

"He's not mad at you!" she coaxed. Tom went to the doorway where his jacket hung on a hook. He put it on and took his truck keys out of a pocket. He went outside and walked abruptly toward his truck. Malinda followed him thinking he was going to her place but heard him say, "If he's going to go crazy with a gun again, I'm getting out of here!"

"Where are you going?" Malinda asked. Tom got in his truck and rolled down the window. He looked downwards at Malinda and said, "I'm going to the city, as far away as I can get from

Brian!" He drove off and left Malinda and his wife standing outside. Malinda could not risk taking more time to call someone else or to drive elsewhere for help. All she could think about was that her husband was going to kill her two children.

She sped back to her house. All the lights were out. The door was jammed shut. Malinda slammed her body against it with all her might. There was a metallic sound and the door swung open. Something flew by her head. Malinda turned on the entrance light and saw that it was a butter knife that had been rammed into the doorframe to keep anyone out. The house was very quiet. Malinda put the kitchen lights on and saw that most of the bulbs of the light fixtures were busted. There were pieces of broken glass all over the floor. The kitchen chairs were turned over like someone had tossed them all around the room. She put on her shoes and walked amidst the broken glass. Once past the kitchen, she saw that the couch chair in the living room was upside down. She went to Nadine's bedroom first but her little girl was not there. She went to Suzanne's room and found the baby's crib empty. Fearing the worst, she went to her bedroom. She turned on the light and saw Brian in a deep sleep with each child asleep in each of his arms. They were all alive! Malinda quietly took each of her children and put them back in their beds. Brian snored and did not wake up.

Malinda wanted to leave the house in shambles to show her husband what he had done, in case he did not remember. However, she and the children often got up before he did. So, before going to bed, she went to the kitchen and cleaned it up.

The next morning, Brian woke and came into the kitchen. He sat in his usual chair and lit a cigarette. Malinda was doing dishes and said, "Look at the lights, Brian." He looked and said, "What happened there?" Malinda made no mention of the fact that he had pointed a loaded shotgun at her; just that he had broken the lights. Often, Malinda was bothered by Tom's comment that insinuated this was not the first time Brian went berserk with a loaded gun.

On moving day Georgette and her husband came to help and said, "I'm glad you two are moving out of here from this den of snakes." She did not know about the gun incident. Malinda told no one and neither did Olive's husband. Brian got a new job and Malinda continued to work part time for an insurance company. Brian drank a lot, mostly with his co-workers and in particular, his boss. Malinda lost hope that Brian would ever change. She feared for her life. Any options to seek help seemed futile; she only hoped there was a God. Having turned her back on religion, Malinda thought *God would never pay attention to me!* She turned to the only person who she thought would be near to God, her mother. She recalled the rosary she found in a coat that was inherited from her mother. Malinda put the rosary under her pillow. Each night she held the item that represented her mother's presence in heaven and said, "Please ask God to make Brian go away so that my children and I can live in peace. I don't ask that he have an accident or die, but that he move out." She prayed to be rescued from the prison she lived in, a death sentence waiting to happen.

Olive and her family also moved to the city. One Saturday afternoon she called Malinda to invite her for dinner and a show. She had tickets to see a country star perform at a fancy inn. Brian was working and was supposed to come home at four o'clock so Malinda could do some grocery shopping. When he did not show up, she called his boss's wife and asked if she could look after the children for a couple of hours. The woman said she was going to be at her husband's warehouse to finish some paperwork. "If you don't mind bringing the girls there, I'll take them to your house afterwards and sit with them until you come back." Olive picked up the children and Malinda. When Malinda entered the warehouse, she saw that Brian was drinking with his boss and a couple of co-workers. She knew that his boss's wife never drank and felt it was safe to leave the children with her. Malinda knew that if she said she was going out for dinner, Brian would keep her from going. She made up a story that she was going to do some grocery shopping with Olive. Out of resentment, she ignored Brian.

Olive drove Malinda back home around eight. She walked up the front sidewalk. Brian waited for her at the front door. She said, "Hello." Then he grabbed her by the left arm and swung her to the floor. She caught a glimpse of his boss and other friends in the living room.

"She won't live to see morning," Brian said. He kicked her with his steel-toed boots. Malinda covered her head with her arms and hands. His boss stepped up and restrained him, saying, "Come on Brian, she's not worth it."

Malinda got up, and Brian put his fist through the front door window. Then he turned to the living room and kicked the children's toys around. He broke Nadine's new dollhouse that he and Malinda recently made together. Malinda interpreted the damage to the playhouse to mean that the children were next in line to be punched. Just then, JJ and his wife dropped in for a visit. They came through the front door and saw the broken glass and blood. JJ asked, "What's going on here?" Brian answered, "Malinda is cheating on me." He turned to Malinda and said, "You met a guy named Carl tonight. I found this paper with his name and phone number on it." Brian reached inside his jean pocket and took out a hand written note with the name Carl on it, along with a phone number. Malinda said, "That paper was on the end table beside the phone. It belongs to our daytime babysitter. She forgot it there yesterday. I kept it for her in case it was an important number for her to have." She then admitted, "I was out with Olive. We went to see Ray Saint-Germaine at the West Town Cabaret. Phone Olive! She'll tell you,"

Brian continued with his jealousy and rejected her alibi. He said with a scornful tone, "You didn't go for groceries, you little slut. You met Carl at a bar!"

"No!" Malinda pleaded, "I'm telling you the truth." Brian grabbed Malinda and pinned her against the wall in the porch. With his other hand he punched a windowpane. Pieces of glass shattered onto the porch and inside the living room. He let go of Malinda and looked at his hand as it bled.

JJ's wife offered to tend the wound, but Brian refused and said, "I love pain and blood." Malinda took the opportunity to run out of the house. She went next door to her neighbour and knocked as hard as she could. She screamed, "Help! Let me in! I need help!" No one answered.

Brian came after her and Malinda ran down the sidewalk. Her neighbour was afraid to answer the door but immediately called the police. Brian caught up with Malinda and grabbed her hair. He pulled her by the hair, back into the house. He threw her on the floor. Malinda broke free and ran upstairs to check on the children. JJ's wife was sitting on Nadine's bed and had Suzanne in her arms. This woman was usually of a quiet nature but this time, she yelled at Malinda, saying, "What are you doing with a crazy man like that!" She packed a couple of bags of the children's clothing.

Malinda said nothing. Meanwhile she looked out the window and saw a police car stopped in front of the house. Everyone in the house sat down quietly. Malinda headed back downstairs. When she turned the corner at the foot of the staircase, she saw the officers talking to Brian. She retreated up a few steps and listened to what they were saying. Brian said, "My wife went to the hotel down the street and on her way home, a stranger chased her down the sidewalk. She's okay now." Then she heard Brian's boss and JJ both back up the story. The police then asked to speak with Malinda. Brian said, "She's upstairs." One policeman walked to the staircase and saw Malinda standing around the corner. The officer inquired if she was Brian's wife. Malinda nodded. Then he asked, "Did you hear what your husband said about what happened to you tonight?" Malinda nodded again. The officer asked, "Is that what happened?" Malinda shook her head hard from side to side and pointed toward the living room. She whispered, "It was him."

The officer asked, "Do you want us to charge anybody?" Malinda shook her head again, this time, less severely. The officer paused for a moment, then said, "We'll drive around the block a few times and stay in the area for a while just to make sure things are alright." After the officers drove away, everyone left but JJ and his wife. Malinda returned to the living room and sat on the reclining chair. She stared in space and thought about how she was defeated.

JJ said to Brian, "Tomorrow, you guys come over for a barbecue." Brian took an empty beer bottle and smashed it against the side table where she was sitting. Quickly he sat on Malinda's lap facing her and held the jagged edges of the bottle to her face. JJ got up and stood beside Brian. He said, "Brian, put that down!" Brian declared, "I'm going to kill her!" JJ remained calm and said, "Nobody's going to kill anyone. Come on, Brian." But Brian did not listen and declared once again, "She's going to die tonight."

JJ became nervous and tried a different approach. He said, "Brian, come on. Tomorrow you, Malinda and the girls will all come to my place and we'll have a barbeque together." Brian replied, "I'll be there and the girls will be there, but Malinda won't see the sunrise tomorrow." He put the broken bottle against Malinda's left cheek. JJ stepped back pulling Brian off Malinda. He held on and yelled, "Run!" Malinda ran out the front door in the hope of finding the police car, but instead she saw JJ's car. His wife was at the wheel with the motor running. Nadine and Suzanne were sitting in the back seat with the bags of clothes. JJ's wife shouted, "Get in!" Malinda jumped in. After a minute or so, JJ walked out and got in the front passenger seat. He was calm, looked at his wife and said, "Okay, let's go." JJ's wife drove away. Malinda thanked her and asked JJ, "What was Brian doing when you left?" JJ answered, "He was sitting in the porch, sulking."

This time, Malinda had no sympathy for the man who promised he would be her husband for the rest of her life. She knew that her marriage had to end or else she, and maybe even her daughters, would be killed. She also knew that without his friends, her husband would not be any more trouble that night.

JJ and his wife owned a three-bedroom house in Laurance. Once there, Malinda was given a camping mat and a blanket to set up in one of the spare rooms. Before Malinda went to bed, she checked in the room next to her and saw Nadine and Suzanne sleeping soundly, snuggled together in a sleeping bag. While lying on her mat, Malinda automatically began to whisper her usual nightly request but then, she realized that her children were asleep, safe and sound and that Brian was now out of the picture. She thought, *the prayer has been answered!* Malinda closed her eyes and, as though talking to God, said aloud, "Thank you for our freedom." A great peace came upon her. Just then, in the darkness, she saw a small bright light that seemed to shine from afar. It looked like the headlight of a train inside a dark and narrow tunnel. Still relaxed and at peace, Malinda felt no confusion and had no doubt that this light was transmitting the message, *you now have a future.* Just then, she saw her inner flame which died down still had a faint light radiating from a mere ember. She knew with certainty, *I'm going to live.*

Nadine was registered to start school in a week's time. Olive was also going through a divorce and was living alone with her son. Malinda asked if she and the girls could move in with them until she found a place to live. Malinda's job entailed working with the public. She had several bruises on her body from that violent night. She asked to meet with her supervisor and told him that she could no longer work there because of her appearance, and also because she wanted to stay with her children to make sure they were safe. Somehow she had found the strength to move toward the unknown, to make changes that would give her children a chance to experience life without violence. Her supervisor informed Malinda about some social welfare and provincial funding that would pay for her divorce. A lawyer was appointed to activate her divorce proceedings. The lawyer was successful to have Brian move out of the house immediately. He returned to live with his parents. Malinda and the children moved back into their home. They were dependent upon government assistance for food but there was no financial assistance to pay for the house mortgage. Soon, the house went into foreclosure. Winter set in and the water pipes froze. The sewage backed up in the basement. The mortgagee hired a real estate professional to list the house for sale. A caravan of real estate agents came to view the house and they were appalled at the conditions Malinda and the children were living in. One of the real estate agents reported the problem to the health department. Malinda thought she would have to move out and worried about where they would live. Fortunately, a provincial housing agency stepped in to help and offered her a low-income house in a complex that was located next to Nadine's school. The rent was paid through a government assistance program. Brian had visitation rights. He picked up his two children once a month for a weekend stay

Malinda faced the reality of her circumstances. She was alone with two very young children. Her self-esteem was in desperate need of repair. Malinda began her recovery by discounting all her husband's negative input in her life. She resolved to try her best. She returned to work at the insurance agency on a part-time basis in the investment division. Much to her amazement, she found contentment in her independence. A confidence that she could manage her affairs alone began to grow and her physical energy increased.

During one of the weekend visits with his children, Brian got drunk. He became aggressive toward the children. The police were involved and Brian was charged. The court found Brian guilty and forced him to attend a support group for alcoholics and was appointed regular visits with a psychiatrist. He was ordered to abstain from alcohol completely and he lost his visitation rights with Nadine and Suzanne.

Malinda identified the things she "didn't want in a man." They included a man who drinks, one who is unfaithful, or mean or cruel, or who did not want to work. Seven months later, Malinda met a man named Gerry. He was an impressive businessman and owned a small land developing company that he had put in dormancy in order to complete his university degree. When they met in April, Gerry was writing the last of his exams. By June, he had re-opened his business. He joined committees and social groups that worked toward the development of a business section in the city.

He gave every indication of caring about Nadine and Suzanne by helping Malinda with the responsibility of their upbringing. He took them to restaurants and bought them new clothes and toys. After two months of dating, Gerry made a proposition to Malinda that she should move into his house and co-habitate with him. Malinda answered, "I'm happy here." Malinda did not want to give up her first taste of independence.

Gerry reasoned, "I have a nice two bedroom house in a quiet neighbourhood. There's plenty of space for you and the girls. My yard is extra large and it's all fenced in so the girls could run around safely in it all they want." Malinda said, "The people here are nice and we help each other out. Nadine just started school nearby."

Gerry stated, "I know the city well and it's not good for the girls to grow up in a welfare compound." He added, "With me, they'll be in a normal neighbourhood and grow up normally." This was no longer about her but about her children. Gerry was able to use that approach to convince Malinda and she agreed to his proposition. She packed up her things once again. On the eve of the move, Gerry announced that he had to work and could not help. Malinda called on her younger brother who owed her a favour.

On the first morning together, Malinda made breakfast while Gerry got ready for work. After he finished eating, he showered and put on a nice three-piece suit. Just before he left for work, he showed Malinda to the living room and said, "There's not much for you to do around here today. You might sew the rip in this carpet seam." Malinda was grateful that her knight in shining armor had finally arrived in her life and she did all she could to please him. Over time, however, Gerry was subtly taking control of her life. More and more, he made critical comments. Her friends were not good enough. He did not like her clothes, so he chose others. He did not like her hairdo, so he recommended a stylist. He convinced her that her job would get her nowhere, and that she should work for him. He controlled the reins of the business. Malinda went along with his plans about the direction the business should take and even which people she should be acquainted with. He coached Malinda on how they should portray themselves as a couple socially. Gerry liked to drink fine brandies. He took Malinda to expensive restaurants and encouraged her to try more sophisticated food and drink. They entertained at home every weekend, using their hospitality with its expensive food and alcohol as a way to make social contacts. Malinda adopted this new sophisticated lifestyle. She joined her common law husband for many public relations galas and events. The only thing that remained unchanged was her smoking. Because Gerry also smoked a pack a day, he never mentioned for her to quit. Keeping up her new appearance made Malinda nervous. She smoked her six cigarettes a day, but before long that number increased to one whole package and sometimes more.

Six months later, Malinda got very ill each time she menstruated. Around three o'clock one morning, she woke up with severe abdominal cramps. She could not sleep and bled a lot, staining the sheets and the bed mattress. She went to the bathroom to clean up. The cramps and bleeding got worse. She sat on the toilet and passed what looked like a piece of chicken liver and fainted. When she regained consciousness, she was on the floor and cold. She took the liver-like blob and wrapped it in cellophane to show her doctor. The next day she phoned her physician and got an appointment the same day. Malinda had seen her doctor several times before with complaints about how difficult her menstrual cycle was. This time, the fainting scared her and she did not mince words. She said, "Doctor, I'm so sick with this now that I am only able to function without cramps one week out of a month." Her doctor referred her to a gynaecologist. Tests revealed that she had a tumour inside her uterus as well as a condition called Endometriosis, which is a collection of fibrous tissues growing on the inner lining of a uterus. Malinda was booked for a hysterectomy. During the operation, a third condition was discovered. The morning after the operation the doctor stood by Malinda's hospital bed and said, "I have good news and bad news. Which one do you want first?" Malinda answered, "The bad, then the good."

The doctor explained, "We had to remove your entire uterus as a result of the excessive amount of endometriosis you had. The good news is that your ovaries were okay and we left them alone. The best news is that the tumour was benign." Weakened by the procedure and after-effects of the anaesthetic, Malinda could not seem to care much about the news. The doctor continued to say that her uterus also revealed scar tissue. Malinda got interested and asked what that was. The doctor explained that scar tissue occurred when a tear or a cut on the body healed and left a permanent mark. Malinda's interest piqued. She probed further and asked, "How did a scar tissue get inside my womb? I don't remember ever having an injury there." The doctor said, "I don't know. It could be from anything."

"Like what, for example?" Malinda continued to inquire.

The doctor answered, "That cannot be determined at this point. It was an old scar that could have been caused by some tearing." Malinda asked, "What could have caused the tearing?" The doctor replied, "It could be a number of things. It will never be known."

"Like what things?" Malinda persisted. "Perhaps like forceps used to deliver a baby." Forceps had been used during Suzanne's birth. Malinda let the subject drop and fell asleep. When she woke up, she thought, *forceps were clamped on my baby's forehead and back of the head when she was already through the birth canal. The forceps would have to reach far inside the uterus to cause the tear which was not the case. Suzanne didn't need rotation; just a slight pull to help get her out.* Her memory of the birth was clear since she chose to have the baby naturally, without the use of pain relievers. How the scar tissue got there remained a mystery.

Darkness Overtakes a Sunny Day

After some years Gerry moved the family to his hometown in Laurance where they bought a new house. Gerry and Malinda worked well together and their business was successful. Little Suzanne was the apple of everyone's eye. She was fun loving. Her platinum blond hair and blue eyes charmed her way into the hearts of everyone who met her. Nadine grew to be a responsible and respected teen. She had an after school job and bought most of her own clothes. Both girls were intelligent and beautiful. Gerry's parents treated the two as their own grandchildren. Gerry was the second oldest of seven siblings. Some lived in Laurance and had children the same age as the girls. Malinda got along well with her new relatives.

At the age of fifteen, Nadine went on her first date with a boy from school. On a hot day in July, Malinda gave permission for Nadine to go swimming at the boy's place. They enjoyed frolic and play and the boy and his friend played a game by having the boyfriend's younger brother dive off their clasped hands while they threw him in the air into the pool. Soon, the boys tried to lure Nadine to stand on their hands and they would whirl her up in the air to dive in the pool. Nadine refused. She remembered that her mother cautioned both her and her sister not to dive in private pools. The two boys continued to ask again and again saying that no harm would come to her and how they did the same to the little boy and nothing bad happened. Nadine finally complied and the two boys joined their hands together and lowered their arms into the water so Nadine could hop on and stand while holding their shoulders as they raised her out of the water. At the count of three the boys flipped Nadine into the air with all their strength. Nadine's thin build was no challenge for two robust sixteen year old boys. Nadine flew high into the air and panicked as she fought to land in the pool without hurting herself. Nadine hit the surface of the water and heard a cracking sound in her neck. She was underwater then floated to the surface with her face down in the water. She could not move. One of the boys swam to her. He flipped her over and said, "What's the matter with you?" Nadine said, "I don't know but I can't move. Get some help!" Her boyfriend shouted to his friend, "Get my parents!" The ambulance was called and Nadine was rushed to a hospital in the city. Malinda was called with the news. She, Gerry and Suzanne drove to the hospital. The drive seemed to take forever. Gerry's cell phone rang. It was Georgette. She received the news and immediately went to the hospital. She asked to speak with Malinda and told her that the news was not good. "Nadine's neck is broken," she said. Malinda asked how Nadine was. Georgette answered, "Apparently she's alright but right now I can't see her because they are putting some kind of special head and neck brace on her." Malinda said, "We're about ten minutes away. Thanks for being with my daughter. We'll be there in about ten minutes. Good-bye."

Gerry dropped off Malinda and Suzanne at the emergency entrance of the hospital and went to park the car. The medical staff directed Malinda to a waiting room. The two boys were there along with their parents. Georgette told Malinda to come sit beside her. "Can I see Nadine?" Malinda asked. Georgette answered, "A nurse came to tell us to wait for the doctor." The room was quiet. No one seemed to want to talk. Malinda was tense but tried not to show it so as not to alarm Suzanne. Gerry walked in. "Come and sit here," said Malinda. "No, I'm going to stand," he answered.

A doctor walked in and asked, "Are the parents here?" Malinda got up and stood beside Gerry. The doctor said, "Your daughter broke her neck at C5. I just put on an apparatus with four metal bars that are screwed slightly into her skull to hold a restraining vest around her chest. She will be wearing the unit for a few weeks to keep her neck from moving. The break was complete and the girl won't be able to walk or feel anything from the neck down." Gerry asked, "What do you mean she won't be able to feel or walk?" The doctor answered, "She won't be able to move her hands, arms and legs. The break in her neck severed the nerves in her spinal cord. The damage is irreparable. In the next four months she may regain some slight movement but not likely." The doctor continued, "You may see her now." A nurse walked in and the doctor left. "Come with me," said the nurse. Malinda turned to get Suzanne. The little girl overheard the conversation and was crying. Malinda came to her and gave her a hug. "Come Suzanne, come with us to see Nadine." The nurse led them to an elevator that took them to the IC unit. There lay Nadine in a bed with a metal contraption that prevented her from moving her head. The nurse said, "She's wearing what we call a halo." Malinda said, "Hi Nadine." Nadine looked like an angel with a suffering halo about her head rather than the radiant gold ones depicted in religious pictures. "They cut up my new bathing suit," Nadine said. Malinda was at a loss of words. She smiled and all that could come out of her mouth was light humour. She said, "You just got rid of all the metal in your mouth from having your braces removed and now you have this metal brace on your head." Nadine's eyes closed. Gerry called to her and asked, "Can you move anything?" Nadine opened her eyes. The nurse said, "She is heavily sedated and probably will be sleeping for several hours. You should go home and come back in the morning. There's no point in staying up all night. Nadine won't be awake." Malinda did not want to go. The nurse said, "You could come back first thing in the morning." They stayed until one in the morning. Nadine was sleeping heavily then Malinda agreed to go home.

The drive home was longer and quieter than the drive to the hospital. Malinda thought about how she asked God every night to keep her daughters from harm. "Don't let them die or have an accident that would permanently hurt them," she had prayed. She could not feel anything for herself. Her emotions shut down as she thought only about what Nadine needed now and in the years to come. When they arrived home, she put Suzanne to bed. She walked to her bedroom and found Gerry fast asleep. Malinda could not go to bed. She was wide awake and waited for the sun to rise so she could go to Nadine. She took a kitchen chair and put it facing outdoors in front of the large picture window in the living room. She could only wait for daybreak. She turned on the radio for company and sat down.

Malinda stared out the window and looked up to the sky. A song by Louis Armstrong called What a Wonderful World began to play. She heard him sing about the blue sky. Malinda looked up at the dark sky and could not see the sparkle of the stars. The clouds and the moon seemed to hang in the dark like purposeless shapes. The splendour of the sky that Malinda always enjoyed failed to move her. She turned her gaze to the full trees of summertime but saw no gentle breeze, no magic charm. Their leaves did not dance and their significance became meaningless. The sacredness of nature could not soothe the devastation of her daughter's accident. As she stared into the emptiness of the night, the anthills of her childhood forest adventures came to mind. Malinda thought about how they existed in a way similar to hers. They built shelters to take care of their offspring. Each adult had responsibilities to contribute to the survival of their young. The tiny creatures gave Malinda a valuable lesson about lasting endurance.

The sun finally rose. Malinda made breakfast and took a shower. Gerry went to work and said he would go to the hospital in the afternoon. Malinda and Suzanne headed for the hospital. Nadine was awake and conscious. Her breakfast was in a tray and unopened. Malinda asked her if she wanted to eat something. Nadine answered, "I'm waiting for someone to feed me." The nurse at the station overheard and said, "Do you want to feed her?" Malinda answered, "Of course." Malinda opened the tray to find Nadine's favourite breakfast which was a bowl of hot cereal except it was cold. Malinda asked where the kitchen was to use the microwave oven. The IC attendant gave her special privileges to the staff kitchen. Malinda spoon-fed her daughter. She felt for Nadine and pretended that she had the courage to do this for her daughter. She had to spoon-feed her while looking at the hardware contraption that was bolted into her daughter's head. After a couple spoonfuls of cereal, Malinda wiped the side of her daughter's mouth with the spoon like one would do when spoon-feeding a baby. Nadine said, "Don't do that." "Sorry," replied Malinda. "I don't want anymore anyway," said the girl.

Nadine spent the next three weeks in the intensive care unit of the hospital. At times she cried and Malinda wiped her tears and her dripping nose.

Nadine was transferred to a Rehabilitation Hospital. On the spinal cord unit, she would spend the next five months undergoing treatment, physiotherapy and occupational therapy. Back home, the house had to be sold because it was a back level split, which could not be remodelled to accommodate a power wheelchair. Malinda's car had to be sold in order to buy an older van that had a manual wheelchair lift. Gerry had no control over circumstances surrounding his stepdaughter's serious injury. He did not have any power over the reality that the accident hit him with. He spent more hours at work and became reclusive at home. One evening Malinda thought it would be good if the two of them went for a walk. She would try to make conversation and perhaps he would start to talk. He went for the walk but remained silent. A few minutes into the walk, Malinda asked him what was on his mind. "Nothing," he answered. She replied, "There's something. I know it. Let me know what it is so you can get it off your chest." To her surprise, Gerry replied, "It's your fault that Nadine had the accident." Malinda expected just about anything to come out of his mouth but that. She was astonished at his answer. She wanted to respond then walk away from him, but instead she managed to control herself. *It's just his anger coming out. He doesn't mean that*, she told herself. "Why do you think that?" Malinda asked. Gerry exploded in reply, "I told you she should stay home that day but *you* let her go swimming!" His accusation reminded Malinda of the times when Brian attacked her verbally just before he got physically violent. She stopped thinking about how the accusation made her feel and found it easier to focus on the care that her daughter needed. Malinda changed the rest of the conversation and focussed on that plan.

· Since Malinda had sole custody of her children, she had to deal with the legal matter of suing for accidental insurance benefits for Nadine. During one of the consultations with her lawyer, she was advised that it would be in the best interest of Nadine for Malinda to marry Gerry. "Even though you lived together for ten years, if you should die, your girls could end up in the custody of your ex-husband," the lawyer explained. That possibility was not something Malinda wanted to risk. She did not want anyone to know about their plan to marry as she was not up for a large celebration. Gerry and Malinda got married secretly and announced the event after the fact. Well-meaning friends and family held a surprise celebration for them. Malinda went through the motions and pretended that her marriage to Gerry was out of love for him when, in fact, she resented him because he refused to retract the accusation that she had caused Nadine's quadriplegia.

The Talisman

With a spinal cord injury there are frequent bladder infections that need to be treated that if left undetected could cause damage to the kidneys. Several other conditions like a sudden rise in blood pressure or swelling of the legs and feet could cause a blood clough and increase the chance of a stroke. Muscle tone, bone shifts, pressure sores and other conditions need to be kept in check. It is also important to have clean air to breath. Depending on how high the neck injury is located, the ability to inhale and exhale is affected. In Nadine's case, the break was her C5 vertebrae. Her ability to inhale remained normal but the ability to exhale was greatly reduced. When she had a cold, she could not cough-up phlegm which put her at risk of getting worse and getting pneumonia. The Association for People with Disabilities (APD) recommended that a fresh air exchange unit be installed in the house and they stressed that both Malinda and Gerry should quit smoking for the sake of their daughter's health. Malinda tried several times in the past to quit but her efforts were always futile. She tried again and again but she was unable to quit – a fact that now made her feel guilty. She supposed the reason was because it was too stressful of a time to win such a huge battle. Every major part of her family's norm was disrupted. The house had to be sold because it was a back split level and could not be renovated to accommodate a power wheelchair. The new house plans needed to be done by a professional architect and verified by the APD for accessibility. The builder rejected some of the adjustments because it interfered with the roof line or foundation so the blue prints traveled back and forth between the APD, the architect and the builder. The house was twice the size of the previous one and twice the price to build it. Nadine was scheduled to come home at Christmas time and the school division in Laurance did not have a wheel chair accessible bus. Malinda was responsible to drive

Nadine to and from her high school. The family sold and moved out of their house. While Nadine was in the hospital, they moved into a temporary place until the new house was finished.

Each day Malinda journeyed to the hospital in the city to be with her daughter. The medical staff trained her to perform several of Nadine's personal care, including some precise nursing procedures. She also made sure to spend time with Suzanne who was 11 at the time. Most relatives, friends and neighbors often forgot about Suzanne because her older sister was the centre of attention and Suzanne lost her spotlight. Malinda made sure to spend every morning with her and be home for when she returned from school. The hours away from her job forced Malinda to bring home some of the paper work. She struggled to keep up with deadlines so Gerry hired a temp at the office.

Malinda contended with local health administrators to provide reasonable hours of care for Nadine. They agreed only to minimal hours of care which was barely enough to justify their efforts. Malinda was told that because Nadine was a minor (under the age of 18) that her mother was responsible for her care.

The parents of the two boys involved in the accident had to be legally pursued to get an insurance settlement for Nadine. Because Malinda had sole custody of her two girls, she was the sole Petitioner and had no choice but to stand up for her daughter's financial future and be at odds with two home insurance companies. If the quadriplegia was caused by an automobile accident, the province's no-fault auto insurance would automatically pay a settlement according to guidelines and without litigation. House insurance claims need to prove that the owners of the swimming pool were negligent otherwise no settlement would be due. The case took two years to settle. At one point, an actuarial was made by a hired accountant and an independent insurance adjuster to arrive at Nadine's future expenses related to her injury. Malinda's lawyer suggested that the insurance companies' coverage although high was not enough to cover for the expenses outlined in the actuarial assessment and recommended she sue personally as well as the amount of the defendants' insurance policy. Malinda was appalled at such a suggestion. When her lawyer asked why she opposed to do that, Malinda answered, "because I like to sleep at night. Those two boys must be going through hell having to deal with what happened to Nadine. I will not now take their home and family dog. We're pursing only the insurance companies - that's all! I know I'm not always going to be around to care for Nadine and that she'll have to somehow work part time to support herself in the future." But a rumour got around that Malinda was indeed suing the two families for their personal goods. Her lawyer emphasized the importance of not talking about the case to anyone because it would jeopardize the case and influence the insurance companies against any offer of settlement. People wanted to know what was going on but since Malinda could not disclose any information many assumed derogatory things. One of the neighbors that attended a church association meeting reported that the parish priest spoke and said that what Malinda and Gerry were doing was not Christian. Others reported that the lawsuit was exploiting her daughter in an attempt to get rich. Another was that Nadine hit the bottom of the pool and ended up with a brain injury which caused retardation. The rampaging allegations and gossip were uncontrollable.

In Malinda's view, it was an undesirable time to even try to quick smoking and she smoked even more so. Finally, she surrendered to the hold that addiction had and she said, "I quit trying to quit. I will probably spend my retirement with an oxygen tank on my back and tubes up my nose."

Shortly after the declaration Malinda was due for a physical exam at the doctor's. During the visit she explained to her doctor how she gave up trying to quit smoking but suddenly remembered a recent commercial on TV that she heard to ask a doctor about a new device to help people who want to quit smoking. The doctor showed her a small package containing little round patches and asked, "Do you want to try it?" Malinda answered, "I haven't done that yet. Yeah, I'll try it." The patches looked like the ones used to repair bicycle tires with; only these contained nicotine. The doctor wrote a prescription and said, "Paste only one a day on your upper arm. If it makes you sick, it's because the dosage might be too strong and make an appointment with me to get a prescription for milder ones." Malinda picked up the prescribed device at a drug store then headed home. There was a cigarette pack on the dashboard of her van. Malinda knew there were two cigarettes left in it. She contemplated smoking them. *It's only two. I'll have one now and the last one, when I get home. After that I'll start on the patch.* She reached for the pack and took a cigarette; closed the pack and tossed it back on the dashboard as she usually did. She held the cigarette between her index and second finger but just as she was about to put it in her mouth an opposing thought came to mind and asked herself, *Does this little thing matter so much to me?*" She held the cigarette vertically and brought it level between her two eyes and shouted, "You! I hate you! You too, you're not my friend. You hurt me! You hurt my lungs. You block my sinuses and I can hardly breathe. Each night I go to bed and the last thing on my mind is how my lungs are sore! You suck energy out of me. You, get out of here." She rolled down the window and threw the cigarette out as far as she could. She was about to roll up the window when she spotted the cigarette pack with the last cigarette in it. She grabbed it and she tossed it out the window as she shouted, "you too! Get out! Get out of my life!"

Malinda used the prescription patches. After three days, they made her sick and she thought, *is this any better than smoking?* I have to use it every day and it feeds me nicotine. What if I get hooked on these in order not to smoke? I still end up with a bad habit. If I can go three days without cigarettes then I have jumped the worst hurdle. An assurance came over her as she continued to think, a thing as small as a stick-on not even one inch big can keep me from a deadly addiction then how much more can I? I am a trillion times bigger than that little patch, she contended. She thought, these are too strong and now I need to return to the doctor and get different ones. What will happen after the six weeks of patches are used? Will I need more? I haven't smoked for 72 hours. These patches make me sick. They are feeding me with nicotine - the same thing that cigarettes do. It's no better. If I am able to quit for three days then I have gone through the worst part. She peeled off the patch from her arm but did not put the next one on. For the balance of the day there wasn't even an inker of neither a craving nor the next day and so on. Malinda never smoked another cigarette again.

Every day after the school run she stopped at the restaurant for a much deserved plate of French fries. Sometimes she ordered desert also. In the evening when she was by herself watching TV, she ate an entire family size bag of potato chips and drank a large tumbler of pop. She put on pounds at a rapid pace. After three months, she was 30 pounds heavier. For the first time in her life she knew what it was like to be overweight.

Two years after her daughter's accident Malinda was overweight. Since kicking the cigarette addiction she delighted herself with some of her favourite foods which were rich in fat and loaded with calories. After going up three sizes in her clothes, she thought, R*ather than start smoking to loose weight, I'll permit myself the weight gain and work on losing it next year.* Gerry became stand-offish when she approached him. Sometimes he walked away. Malinda was unhappy as she thought; *I expected a better reward for breaking that horrible cigarette habit other than weight gain and a husband that finds me unattractive.*

When Nadine turned 18, Malinda immediately called the health aide department to tell them that her daughter was now an adult and needed more hours of care. The department added some hours of care for Nadine but would not provide respite for Malinda. The new house was nice and roomy. Nadine received an insurance settlement and she bought a new van that was electronically equipped and accommodated a power wheelchair. People saw that Malinda did not sue the respondents personally but the gossip still went on. Nadine completed high school and registered at a University to get a degree in Education. Malinda had to drive her but that summer, Nadine bought her own van and got it converted. Then, she did the unthinkable. she went to Toronto to get specialized driving lessons that her province did not offer. After a few months, Nadine was driving herself and by herself to the University. Although nothing returned the way things were before Nadine's accident, the dust had finally settled.

For two years Malinda stretched the limits of her physical abilities from having to move twice and all the other demanding matters. Malinda's exhaustion gave way. One day she stayed in bed all day and got up only when Nadine called for assistance. When the task was over, she went to the washroom and returned to bed. When she returned to bed she cried until she fell back asleep. She lost all will to fight and felt herself giving up and spiralled into a dark place that felt like a pit. It was then that she encountered an old familiar theme and came face to face with the resentfulness against her father. That pit was so deep and far from anyone that

Malinda had no concerns about what anybody thought of her. She laid blame on her deceased father with run away thoughts. *My own father did not love me, how can I expect another man to love me. There's something that makes me unlovable*, she surmised. The pit felt like a place where unlovable people are thrown in. Charges against God depicting how He had sent her more than her fair share of problems reeled out. The voices of well meaning people echoed in the dungeon about how God does not send you more than you can handle and she exasperated, *well, He sent me more than I can handle*. She noted how Suzanne became a rebellious and an incredibly unmanageable 14 year old. She pointed out that her marriage was failing and the reality of facing another divorce was catastrophic for her and she could not deal with it. There was nothing left of Malinda to look after the whole lot.

It was the middle of the day when Gerry walked into the bedroom and bent forward over Malinda and woke her up. When she slowly opened her eyes she did not remember how many days she had been sleeping. Gerry's face was all she could see. He said, "I just want you to be happy." Malinda could only respond to his want with, "I can't." Gerry left the room and Malinda felt sorry for him that she couldn't make herself or anyone else happy. She questioned why she had been attracted to him. When they met, he seemed to teach her everything she needed to know. Now, with a growing awareness of how much she allowed him to control every aspect of her life, to dominate and criticize her, Malinda also realized that in the process, she let go of every bit of her own social and financial independence. The words, "I can't," returned and continued to occupy her mind. Other thoughts and worries vanished. Then an unusually confident whisper came out and announced, "You can and you will." As though it was a dream she saw herself at the bottom of a dismal cave and in it was what looked like one piece of smouldering coal - the remains of that fire within that once fuelled her drive was suffocating by the load of setbacks. Suddenly there a tiny spark appeared and Malinda drifted into a deep and peaceful sleep. When she woke up it was morning. She managed to get out of bed and stayed up to do some light household chores. She returned to bed and rested intermittently throughout the day. It was as though that tiny amber of light within was fanned and began to glow once more. Her broken life began the stages of reconstruction. That day Malinda took the first steps toward the process of cancelling the *I cants*, with *I can and I will*.

Each step of the way moved Malinda toward an increase in confidence. In baby steps Malinda's self view was changing. When she felt bad about her extra pounds, she reminded herself her victory over smoking. When criticizing her looks and telling herself that she was getting old and ugly, she boldly rebutted, "but I quit smoking." The one triumph became her talisman. When she thought of herself terrible at parenting Malinda repeated like a mantra, saying, "But I quit smoking." She talked back to her fears and negative thoughts with something positive.

Malinda gave up drinking hard liquor and limited herself to just one beer or a bit of wine during a meal but not to get drunk. When friends walked in with cases of beer and bottles of whiskey, Malinda remained sober. She truly believed that it was her prerogative not to get drunk and that friends would not mind but they disapproved of her new drinking style saying, "There's nothing wrong with having a few drinks. We're all business people and we're just de-stressing." When she refused a second drink, they said, "Why are you being such a snob?" It was then that Malinda reached the conclusion that those types of friends only liked her if she got drunk with them. Malinda remembered what she said to her two last cigarettes, *you are not my friend.... You hurt me*, that the same words could be said about those friends. Family members that Malinda used to get drunk with also disapproved. When she politely passed on drinking, one of them sarcastically remarked that she was a miss goody two-shoes. Eventually Malinda drifted apart from drinking relationships and felt that she had no real friends.

Malinda met with her general practitioner, Dr. Fiji, whom she had been seeing now for over 20 years and vociferously proclaimed, "I think I have bipolar disorder." Dr. Fiji was calm and asked, "Why do you think that?" Malinda answered, "Because I hate everybody. I want to lock the door of my house and unhook the phone but I can't because those are Nadine's lifelines." Dr. Fiji asked, "What makes you want to do that?" Malinda answered, "Because I have a lot of problems and some people say and do things that leave me dumbfounded." The doctor asked, "What are your problems?" Malinda spoke angrily and counted on her fingers as she said, "First, my younger daughter has become a problem at school. I get called every week about something she did to irate her teachers. Her grades have dropped drastically this year. She drinks and I think she is taking drugs because her eyes are glossy when she comes home from partying. I found an altered glass bottle that looks like some kind of pipe to smoke up with. We argue every day and the last time it turned physical. Two, I have no more friends because I stopped getting drunk with them." Then Malinda raised her voice and said, "I don't want to see or talk to anybody. People say ridiculous things to me and about me, like, how I intend to spend Nadine's insurance money on myself! Another one told me that God didn't send me more than I can handle! I know of some people that can't handle even half of what I have to. When they say that, it sounds like God crippled my child! It's so stupidly ridiculous." Malinda moved forward to the edge of her chair and criticized how she had to contend with health officials. She boasted, "They provide barely any help for Nadine and no respite time for me. I'm exhausted!" Then she took a deep breath inward and finished by saying, "This is what discourages me the most. My husband isn't there for me and blames me for Nadine's accident. I know that I'm headed for another divorce." Malinda looked frightened and stared straight into Dr. Fiji's eyes. "It's not like me to hate people. I want to see a psychiatrist," she demanded. The doctor remained calm and spoke. "Malinda, you asked me a couple of times already in the past if you inherited bipolar disorder because it appears in your family history. I told you that you did not." Malinda quickly contested, "how do you know? I've never been tested!" the doctor answered, "Because if you had the illness, then you would not readily admit it." But Malinda pressed the doctor further and asked. "Can you tell by a blood test?" With care and patience, the doctor spoke gently and affirmed, "Your problems are all real and you are trying to handle them all at the same time. It is better if you take one problem and deal with that one before you deal with the next one." Malinda listened attentively. She blew out a loud exhale and moved comfortably to the back of her chair. Her eyes lit up and with a smile of gratitude, she nodded and stated, "I can do that!"

Part 2 – Quest for Love

After Malinda rated her problems from most to least important, she asked Gerry to move out, and suggested that they get counselling before deciding if the relationship should end. Shortly after which Gerry moved in with a woman from his work and served Malinda with divorce papers. After 14 years, her marriage and business relationship with Gerry was over. She settled to own half the house with Nadine plus two years of child support and alimony payments of $1,100.00 a month but claimed no part of the business that she helped build. When Malinda became concerned that the townspeople would again judge her for breaking-up and not standing by her husband, she was able to follow with the thought, "But how will it look for him?"

Malinda was careful not to return to the habits she used to cope with stress so she went out for a walk each day. The exercise felt good and she took up jogging and felt even better. While she ran, she thought a lot about the past and how her present efforts made her healthy. The other problems in her life fell into perspective and she resolved them one by one. Gerry did not want her at work but that didn't devastate her as much as she thought it would. She started to reflect about her future and concluded that she had a chance to do what she liked and not because somebody liked her to do. Her new found independence made her hungrier for more. Her new lifestyle choices gave her get-up-and-go, physically and mentally but emotionally, she wanted to learn how to heal from past hurts. She went to second hand shops and the library to look for some self help books on the subject. She read that no one could feed her emotional nurturing better than her own self. Knowledge about thoughts, feelings and actions intrigued her. It caused her to evaluate areas of her own mental and emotional self. She was looking for answers in order that her past won't continue to repeat itself. Her quest to find out what real love was birthed the idea to pursue a career in counselling and help other women become responsible and heal from past hurts.

She went to both universities in the city and inquired about taking a course in counselling that specialized in emotions. Both places suggested that she should study those topics on her own while completing the counselling course. Malinda submitted an application as a mature student and paid a tuition fee of $900.00 at the continuing education division.

Malinda was on cloud nine and thought, *if I live as long as my life's expectancy that means that I still have 40 more years to fill. There's a whole life ahead of me to live again.*

A week later an administrator from the university phoned and explained that her application was declined and her cheque will be refunded to her. The reason was that one of the requirements was that she had to either be employed or work as a volunteer in the counselling field. Malinda could not understand that in order to get the education necessary to get the job, she had to already have the job. She inquired at several counselling centers about volunteering but the only position offered to her was to mop floors. The dream led her to a dead end. She was newly recovered from lying in bed all the time and was cautious about overdoing things. She valued her health and thought she could handle a part time job though it was not going to be easy to get because Gerry refused to give her a work reference. She thought, *how am I going to submit a resume that looks like I was out of workforce for the past 14 years?* She searched the classified section of the city newspapers when one of the ads leaped out of the page. It read, *Become an Emotional Response Therapist. Private counselling firm is offering a two year course with practical application with supervision from a licensed psychiatrist. Tuition and program fees applicable.* Malinda phoned immediately and got an appointment for an interview. She filled out an application and answered questions in front of a panel consisting of a board member, the director and a psychiatrist. They said they'd contact her within ten days with their decision. She knew not to raise her expectations too high this time and continued to look for part time work. Ten days went by without a phone call from the centre. A couple of days later Malinda picked up her mail and there it was – a letter from the centre. Her heart was pounding and hoping for positive results but prepared for rejection. *If they rejected me, I won't fall apart*, she told herself.

This time she was accepted! The centre was looking for someone that was mature with the life experience that Malinda had but the fact that the panel was impressed with was that Malinda initiated a healing journey in the right direction. For those reasons she was chosen. The centre operated a wellness division. The letter stated that she was a qualified candidate for the programme of study.

For the first year Malinda traveled to and from the city in the evening to attend the classes. She did as the university adviser had recommended and supplemented her studies with other books. She continued to spend time at the library and in bookstores and read many books on emotional know-how. She found the topic fascinating. It was remarkable how she could read and understand the subject matter with ease. Unlike the school years of the past when she could not understand more than a couple of lines of printed material, now she felt capable of being educated. Malinda specialized on the correlation between emotions and abuse victims and built a repertoire on domestic abuse and relatable characteristics.

Nadine and Malinda got along well. The household was peaceful and quiet which made studying an ideal place to learn. Malinda studied along side her daughter. She was pepped up and documented hundreds of pages of notes and compiled them in separate categories on her computer. Sometimes the material stimulated emotional reactions when she read case studies that resembled her own past hurts.

There were six other students that attended the course. The practicum commenced into the second year of the course. To prepare for the real thing, the students participated in role-playing exercises. Once when the students paired up to act as a counsellor Malinda volunteered to be the client. The acting clients were asked to make up something that would cause emotional pain and relate it to the acting counsellor. Malinda thought *this is going to be a breeze; after all, I'm just acting.* She chose to tell about Nadine's accident and how that was hurtful as a mother to live through. Malinda stated, "When my daughter was in the hospital," then she choked up and broke out in real tears. Someone handed her a tissue. She was embarrassed and kept her head down as she blew her nose. The acting counsellor said, "That's something that hurts you a lot. You love your daughter." Malinda couldn't speak but nodded as she wiped her tears away. "It's alright to cry. Those are healing tears," the instructor added.

The course taught that feelings seek resolution and need to be expressed. To provide good Counselling services was a responsibility Malinda owed to herself as well as to her future clients. With a private counsellor, she began the process of first mourning the death of her parents. Tears Malinda could not cry at their funeral came out of hiding and she finally grieved the loss of both parents and her valued brother and his wife.

The extra reading gave details of some exercises to enhance emotional healing; one of which was to write in a journal about anything and everything she ever felt, good or bad. On the first page she wrote to Brian: *I remember that night as if it just happened. When you kicked me while I was on the floor, I felt like the lowest form of life. I wish I could beat you up. If I could, you would have had a serious licking and you would know how it feels. We had nothing and you left me with nothing but all the responsibility to raise our daughters. Because you're lazy and don't work, you get a free lawyer. I have to pay for mine and you know that. You brought me to court on every little whimper you could make up. You did that just to make my life hellish. For years after the divorce, you continued to hurt me.*

My family wrecked my wedding night. I wish I had the guts to tell them off instead of acting like a door mat. I wish I had the guts to get away from them and leave town like I wanted to do. Now, I am going to learn how to do that. It's not too late!"

When she put her feelings down on paper, she didn't think about what anything sounded like or if anybody approved or not. It was her feelings in the rawest form. After she finished the page, she looked at it and realized that after the expression of anger, a release came over her and power immerged. The past was expressed and strength for change evolved. As the hurts emerged the pain made her cry. She studied how to express certain feelings and use more descriptive language and used words like abandoned, ridiculed, humiliated, deceived, and rejected. The ambiguous feelings were identified more precisely. Sometimes it felt like a knife was twisting inside her gut but she knew it was pain that had been avoided for much too long and it had to be released in a safe manner. The pages of her journal provided such an avenue. She labored through the exercise two or three times a week. The emotional snap shot of her past was emotionally draining work that tired her physically as well. Malinda realized how she got rid of emotional pain by focusing somewhere else and avoided a relationship problem in the hope that it would rectify itself. The numbing effect was one that she most used. A bad circumstance was handled by smoking cigarettes, eating or getting drunk and how she could not stand silence where she could hear her thoughts. A radio or TV had to be on when she was by herself in the house. That only lasted until she could find somebody to visit or have them visit. With help from her counsellor, she was able to uncover that those choices only caused a spiralling effect which lead to a worsened situation. In the past, when things got out of control, rather than taking responsibility and resolve the problem, she waited to be rescued. The mess deteriorated her health and the damage was emotional and mental as well as physical.

Eventually Malinda unloaded her old baggage of blaming the people that hurt her in the past for the choices she made in the present. For that to happen, a radical change of thinking had to occur. She forced her brain to think differently. A simple exercise taught in Driver Education to look at where you want to go rather than look at the object you are trying to avoid seemed simple enough but for Malinda her mind was programmed to stare at the past and list things to avoid. She realized that her way was sure to lead her straight for the ditch again. It sounded easy to do but Malinda's mind was deeply programmed. To look to where she wanted to go was not easy. When she spotted a "bad boy" and magnetized toward him she had to look the other way and forget about him. Before she could find real love she had to know what it looked like which was what her healing journey was all about. That type of change had to happen from the inside out. The prior quest, Malinda thought, was to get love from things or people. The instructor at the centre used a lot of common phrases to emphasize a point. One of which was that you cannot give what you don't have. Malinda readily admitted what she didn't have – love; and realized that she had to have love. Not the type that made her desperate in the past but this love was being nurtured from within to eventually grow and continue to grow for the rest of her life. That's what she wanted first.

Another common phrase the instructor used was one that Malinda never heard before which was, in order for something different to happen, one must do something different. The definition of insanity is to keep doing the same thing over again and expect a different result. The cliché resounded loud and clear.

In the past Malinda went to her older siblings for advice but when she did that, the outcome was always the same. They talked to her much in the same way that her father did. The help session always resulted in feelings of inadequacy. She believed what they said was true. Why not? They were her gurus. The insanity was to go to her dysfunctional family for advice on how to not be dysfunctional. By reaching out and getting professional help her personal claims of disapproval was loosing power.

In her journal, she wrote about the time when Gerry said something demeaning to her. His words were identical to what her father would say. Malinda yelled at him and told him off. She quickly headed to her bedroom and closed the door and thought that Gerry would barge in to push her around like Brian did. When she could not hear any pounding footsteps coming down the hallway she stood in the middle of the room and didn't know what to do. She was alone in unfamiliar territory. Her thinking went astray, *"What do I do with this kind of fight?"* she questioned. She was left alone in the room with a stranger - herself. The stillness was scary and Malinda broke the silence and continued the fight; only it was not with Gerry but with her deceased father. Out of respect for the dead Malinda kept the resentments she harbored against him quiet. In one burst she declared out loud, "This is your entire fault. I end up with men who don't care about me; Men who don't love me. Because *you* didn't love me, I don't know how to get love." Alone in the room, she wanted to get back at her father. She returned to confront Gerry to tell him that their relationship was over. As she did to her two last cigarettes, she told him to leave and never come back. He refused and ignored her with silence. It was yet another thing her father used to do to her when pretending she was not there. It made Malinda feel invisible. Malinda was experiencing an older sensation but with someone in the present. She wrote that she had chosen to be with someone who was emotionally unresponsive and aloof. The old was familiar and, like a magnet, that was where she habitually would be drawn toward.

Malinda identified that her reaction set off by a present event that simulated a past incident. The combination of emotional distance and aloof mirrored her father's behavior and unleashed the hurt and anger which Malinda stored away at the time. With a similar romantic partner Malinda attempted to fix the relationship with her father and make it right. The need for parental acceptance was relived with the man in her life. Malinda unknowingly worked hard to get her lover to give her the love she yearned for all her life. A victory would prove that she was wanted and worthy of love. It would negate all feelings of inadequacy held since her childhood.

Malinda opened her eyes and put her experience in perspective. She rationalized intellectually rather than emotionally. The academic knowledge brought her closer to answer the question, what was real love? The self help books described certain characteristics of a behavior style referred to as "co-dependent." Malinda checked every behavior and realized that every romantic relationship she had was birthed from this so called co-dependency. The repeated attempt to get a man to love her became an addiction and, like an addict, was afraid of not getting a fix; only her drug of choice was love.

Malinda learned some hard lessons that were necessary to prevent past mistakes from repeating. If not, the past would keep on being the present and the emotional pain would never leave. The hard work paid off some immediate benefits. Malinda used the new knowledge not only for herself but also to help both her daughters achieve greater self-esteem and a mutually supportive relationship developed between them. Both girls were affected by Malinda's two divorces and the changes that took place after Nadine's accident. Malinda learned to let go of negative self-image through the criticizing messages of her past and replaced them with self-parenting encouraging ones. With help from her counsellor, Malinda and her daughters committed to love and respect each other. Suzanne moved back in. Emotionally mother and daughters became stronger and happier.

A video Malinda watched on the subject taught that in order to have healthy relationships one had to *become* healthy. She began to fight against her need to have a man. It was the first step in finding a way out of co-dependency.

The first person Malinda needed to learn to love was herself. She aggressively confronted the old lies that were programmed in her belief system and realized that her past was not her present. One of the major issues she confronted was that when she wanted something for herself, it was considered to be selfish. Malinda did not know how to administer self-love. In a love relationship, she only knew to do what somebody else wanted or needed. She did things for people in order to be liked. Even getting drunk with people was a way to maintain friendships. Co-dependency made her an imitation and robbed her from being genuine. The efforts and energy Malinda put in to get others to love her was physically and emotionally tiring. Eventually she fell apart. Piece by piece she sewed herself back together. The first stitch was the beginning of a process to get *her* to love her.

The negative self-judgments that ruled her life would not give up power easily. When Malinda identified a fault-finding thought she replaced it with a kind one and sometimes put a voice to the new declaration. By saying the uplifting statements aloud until the modification became subconsciously habitual, it replicated the fashion in which Malinda adopted disapproving remarks to be true. The exercise made her realize just how much put-downs from her past bombarded her mind throughout the day. For instance, one morning she was flipping eggs in a frying pan and was careful not to break the yokes when she thought, *you can't do anything right*. She identified the thought and stopped what usually followed which was that the yokes would break. It was uncomfortable to say, "Those are my father's words. I am not to blame for how he spoke to me. The eggs will do whatever eggs do." Malinda wrote an affirmation that had to be no more than three brief statements and posted it on her computer monitor and on the bathroom mirror. Each time she looked at it, she said, "I am confident; I can say no, I have a right to my opinion." Malinda nick-named the destructive thoughts, "chatterbox." When she could hear the chatterbox she imagined that it had a button and turned it off. Repetitive affirmations became part of the healing curriculum. Even so, the self-assured statements took time before they had a positive effect.

Sessions with her counsellor was a venue where Malinda could express her thoughts and feelings in a safe environment where a lot of anger was expressed. The subject of religion often came up. Although Malinda disagreed with some of the Church's actions, she still fundamentally believed in the underlying faith structure. During one of the sessions she told about how she did not believe in religion but still had her daughters baptized and received the sacraments of First Communion, Confession and Confirmation. Also, after acquiring a legal divorce from Brian she applied to the Catholic Archdiocese to have the marriage annulled by the church. She was told that the procedure would nullify the marriage completely as though it never took place. She expressed to her counsellor how she found the reason silly and asked, "If my marriage to the father of my children is invalidated, then wouldn't that make my daughters illegitimate?" Her counsellor did not answer her question but asked, "Why did you apply for an annulment?" Malinda answered, "Without it I can't remarry in the church." Malinda continued to express the frustrations she had with an ordeal about when a priest from the diocese asked her a series of questions that she was embarrassed to talk about the marriage's sexual tendencies and that she was uncomfortable to have the discussion taped. As part of the requirements she was asked to give five names of people that were close to her and Brian and would agree to be witnesses of the relationship and have their observances also tape-recorded. Malinda explained that although she mistrusted them with the tapes, she did it anyway. "The testimonies were sent to the Vatican in Rome for a decision," voiced Malinda, "and who knows who listened to them and where the tapes are now?" she continued. She took a sip of water and continued to talk. "After two more years, the archdiocese contacted me. They wanted me to come in and sign some documents. A nun took me to an office and explained that after these papers were signed there would be a waiting period before a certificate of annulment would be issued. The nun said, "Until such time, continue to abstain from Eucharistic communion during mass." I asked what she meant and the nun answered, "Unless a divorced person receives special permission from our office through your parish priest, you have to continue to refrain from communion. Once the annulment is granted and a certificate of annulment is issued, you can take communion again." I got nervous and said, "I've been taking communion. I didn't know I wasn't supposed to do that." The nun responded, "Well, you have to wait."

I didn't dare say it, but thought, *if Christ died for me like your teachings communicate, then I can't picture him telling me to leave his dinner table because I am divorced. Also, if he knows everything, then he would know that I was beaten both physically and spiritually and yet tried so very hard to make the marriage work. He would know how much I regret this failure. He would know that I feared for my children's life.* When the meeting was over, I pleasantly left and buried the anger, that is, until now.

The counselor commented, "Is there more about this procedure that angers you?" Malinda answered, "Yes. A few months later, the same nun called to tell me that the final papers were ready for me to sign and that although the annulment is free of charge, the church would appreciate a donation. I asked her how much of a donation was expected and she said, $200.00. Then I told her that I didn't need the annulment after all. Ever since then, religion is a road that I never want to ever walk again."

On The Road Again

Malinda felt confident enough to begin dating and met a widower named Charles through the personal ads of a newspaper. Charles had no children. He lived alone with a little poodle named Coco. The little dog was a burden to him but Charles said that he could not give the dog away because it belonged to his wife that had passed away a year prior. After two dates, Charles offered to take Malinda on a Caribbean cruise at his expense. He took out his wife's expensive jewellery and said, "Malinda all my wife's nice things would be yours and you would never have to work again." "I have lots of money," he added. The promises made it particularly difficult to dismantle the old habit of marrying someone for the wrong reasons. Malinda thought how nice it would be to not have financial worries but she turned him down and remained on course. Charles then took a stab at her emotions. Another time, he brought Malinda to see his house. Coco ran to greet them. When Malinda sat on the couch, Coco jumped on her lap. Charles said, "He needs a new mommy." Malinda ignored his comment and said, "Your house is very nice." Charles went to the kitchen to get Malinda a pop drink. Malinda petted Coco and felt sorry for the little dog. She felt guilty for not wanting to be his new mommy. To commit and provide companionship to Charles and the little dog would help them both. A book she was reading offered a gage to help identify an action based on guilt feelings. To fill someone else's need is a commendable thing and necessary in a romantic relationship but not in a way that would hurt the giver. Malinda thought, I would be filling Charles' need in a way that would hurt me." Not in a violent way but in a way that Malinda would once again move away from her dreams and live for her husband in the way that he wanted. Malinda allowed her feelings but this time, rather than commit, she ended the relationship.

The more Malinda learned to better relate with her feelings, the more she wanted to share her newfound knowledge with others, particularly women and teach them to be responsible. It was like her dormant dream to sing on a stage was revived but with a slight difference. Instead of singing a message of love, she would be telling it. It was an underlining force that compelled her to pursue that dreaded stage. Only one thing would stand in her way which was fear. She remembered how nerve wracking it was to build up enough courage to climb the steps and stand in front of an audience. At the same time she also remembered how the passion to live that dream made her put one foot in front of the other and felt the fear but did it anyway. Looking back, she realized how the love of singing won over the fear and gave courage to go ahead and perform. Malinda used that past experience as a useful tool.

She called a second stage housing complex nearby that provided direction and counselling for women. The women and their children there moved out of their domestic violence situation. She called and asked the director if they would be interested in her help as a group facilitator. She found out it held weekly support groups but no one offered assertive training like the kind Malinda proposed. The idea was welcomed and Malinda was scheduled to facilitate weekly sessions. The experience would help her test the reaction of a group audience.

Even with the many books on abuse and everything else she learned from her course studies, she was nervous and couldn't choose a topic for her first appearance. She went to see Mr. Hilton at the counselling center for help. He said that she should just talk about her own life experience. Malinda was snappy and asked, "Then why did I study so much and read so much if all I have to do is talk about me? Was it all for nothing?" The instructor smiled and said, "of course not. Your knowledge is the repertoire of your talk, and not the star. As you speak you will find that knowledge is what you use to describe your story."

Just in case Mr. Hilton was wrong and the women at the shelter would be board when listening to her life story, Malinda brought along one of the help books to teach as a backup plan. She put together other materials and her notebook, placed them in a briefcase and headed to the shelter. Since the facility was nearby Malinda thought to walk rather than drive because there was a park along the way which she could use to walk across to help her relieve the tension she felt about her first appearance. When she arrived at the shelter, the receptionist brought her inside a tiny kitchen that had been converted as a counselling room for the clients. Inside were seven women that sat on a couple of couches and some chairs. The director introduced herself and told Malinda she could use the kitchen table to put her materials on. There was a fresh pot of coffee brewing on the kitchen counter and a plate of cookies. The director invited the women and Malinda to pour themselves a cup of coffee after which the session would begin. Malinda's first words were that of gratitude as she thanked her audience for their warm welcome. Then she went on to tell about how this experience would help her to further a career as an advocate and public speaking to help other women. She placed her briefcase on the table and displayed the help book and passed around a brief about her life's most tragic moments. Malinda took the book and read a passage that triggered a memory from her past. She shared a little on how she got rescued the night when Brian threatened to kill her. Then she talked about why and how she began a healing journey. The women were attentive. One of which was only 21 and the oldest was 62. Malinda looked at their faces and she could see hope in their eyes and felt their courage. All had to leave their homes and went to a first stage shelter before arriving here. This place of refuge from a violent husband or boyfriend was the only option left for these women. Most of them had been rescued by police. Most of them left everything behind except their children and the clothes they had on during a violent incident. Some community charities and a city food bank donated food and clothing to the women. Each was given a modest apartment to live in safety with their children. Malinda remembered and understood what it was like to suddenly be homeless without notice.

When the hour was up, Malinda encouraged the women to first view the shelter not only as a safe place to live but also to use the time there as an opportunity to gain knowledge and use the counselling services as first steps toward their own healing journey. She packed up her things and thanked everyone for their friendliness. While she walked back through the park, she was filled with a feeling of fulfillment from giving of herself by sharing her story and how she received more than she gave. Malinda's stage fright got reduced that much more and volunteering became the engine that kept repeated, "I think I can, I think I can!

Malinda looked forward to the hour at the shelter and gave her best to the women. She told the group that they were lovable because she loved them. She also said that she was a work in progress on a venture to heal from domestic abuse. Malinda walked to the shelter to clear her mind of clutter from her own personal issues and from the several hours of planning for the weekly presentation. The walk through the park mirrored her childhood forest. On her way to the shelter, one day, something strange happened. Captured by the clear blue sky and a warm breeze that made the oak trees hustle their leaves, a word came to mind. It was only one word but it represented a whole other topic than the one in her briefcase filled with papers and books from the hours spent to perfect her chosen theme. She still presented her own topic but kept the word she received along the way in the back of her mind. When she spoke to the group or when one of the women had a question, there was always an opening to bring up the subject that came to her in the park. The women commented that it was the very subject they talked about during their morning support group with the director. One of them asked if the director and Malinda consulted with each other before Malinda's visit. The director answered, "I'm just as surprised as you are! I have an ethical obligation to not disclose what is discussed during group." The women were not convinced and one of them asked Malinda, "Then how come you remarked about what we talked about this morning?" Malinda thought that if she answered with the truth that the women would ridicule her and the director would no longer welcome her. From her own experience she knew that a battered woman could develop the sixth sense of spotting a phoney should she make up a lie. She opted to use the mantra, "feel the fear and do it anyway." Malinda proceeded to tell them that the squirrels, birds and the trees in the park had a calming effect and caused an idea to mention a different theme. Having no other explanation, she told a story about how her mother had that strange ability and when she was asked how she knew, she answered, "A little birdie told me." Malinda said, "Do you think I inherited this from my mother?" The women enjoyed the story. They smiled and that day Malinda felt that they accepted her completely. During the following week's presentation, the women said that when they were told that they had to come to these classes that they opposed the new program. One of the women said, "I got up this morning and thought, hurray! Today is Malinda's class! Now I can't wait to attend." After a few weeks, Malinda and the director noticed a change in the appearance of the women. Their eyes that were visibly dull now sparkled. Their deadened eyes returned to life. The director commented that she wished she could take a before and after picture of each women and show them the difference from when they first arrived at the shelter. The women taught Malinda that hope can be seen in a person's face.

The president of the shelter home named Richard was interested in Malinda. He was recently divorced and had two grown children. He was also a successful insurance broker. Richard asked Malinda out and she accepted. Richard behaved properly and treated Malinda with gentleness and care. Over the course of some weeks, Malinda admired his steady and pleasant personality. He was calm, polite and sympathetic toward vulnerable persons. He dealt with life with a logical approach. They got along well and never fought. After a year of seeing one another, they bought a condominium in the city and moved in together. Nadine was twenty-one. She did not wish to move to the city so Malinda prepared her by teaching her how to look after a household and manage expenses. Her cousin Cathy moved in with her and additional heath care hours were approved for Nadine. Suzanne gave birth to a baby boy and lived with the child's father.

Months prior to Darren's funeral Malinda told her counsellor that Nadine noticed that her fingers twitched constantly. The counsellor suggested that the uncontrollable spasms may be related to anxiety and recommended relaxation exercises. Malinda picked up a book on the subject and used the described treatment technique. It involved sitting up straight on a chair in a room by herself and remove all distractions. The goal was to reach a relaxed state of mind. Malinda got an antique chair that she refinished and afterwards never knew what to do with it. It became her relaxation exercise chair. She placed it in a corner of her bedroom. At the time she lived with Nadine and told her what she was doing and that she could not answer the phone nor receive any visitors for about a half hour. Malinda closed her bedroom door and sat on her chair. First, she focused on her big toe to relax it but the old fear of being alone in the quietness consumed her mind. In a room by herself with the door closed, even if it was in the middle of the afternoon, Malinda was scared that something or someone was lurking about. She fought the fear with her mantra and pictured a lovely place in a forest and the fearful thought dissolved.

By closing her eyes she eliminated any visual distraction like the dark walk-in clothes closet which someone could be hiding in could interrupt the exercise. When she tried to focus on her toes, her mind wondered all over the place as fear felt like it bounced about throughout her body. At night Malinda always slept with the covers over her head to avoid seeing shadows that could scare her. It was a silly thing to do but she wished that one day she could sleep normally and breath fresh air with her head out from underneath layers of blankets. Although she knew that a blanket could not save her from harm it created a feeling of *out of sight-out of mind.*

The book instructed another visual picture like a large room in disarray that represented her worrisome thoughts. Then to imagine removing herself from the room and picture a cleaning company coming in to empty the room of all its furnishings until there were only the bare walls and floor left. Repeating this exercise every day Malinda gradually became comfortable in the stillness of her own bedroom. She pictured the roof of the house opening and a large suction vacuumed out all the dirt and dust away. The pretend cleaning staff returned to wash and polish the floor. The first few attempts at the exercise produced a picture of the room with its disinfected walls and gleaming black and white chequered flooring. At that stage of the exercise Malinda began to relax every stitch of her body until she was totally calm. After only two weeks, the finger twitching stopped. She continued the exercises on a daily basis. After some time, Malinda became more serene and dealt with life in a more rational way.

These were the years of Malinda's life which preceded her attendance at Darren's funeral. When Malinda sang Amazing Grace that day, her voice came from a place of giving and not trying to impress people to receive recognition. The song that she and her brother sang echoed throughout the congregation and reverberated like it was travelling right through the walls of the church straight up to God in heaven! Then the priest blessed the coffin that Darren lay in. The pallbearers gathered around and lifted the coffin and proceeded to walk out slowly. The family and then the congregation followed behind down the isle. In the cinema of her mind, Malinda played out her past as it mused with her present which collided with her future. She was at a crossroad. She looked at the coffin being carried away and thought, *Darren ended his life while mine is headed somewhere else; only I don't know where it will take me.*

Part 2

Quest for Love

Women were calling to book counselling appointments with Malinda. The director of the shelter for women suggested that she offer a course to the public. Malinda knew it was the next step to take. The director called a few contacts and a public school offered Malinda a classroom at no cost to run an Assertive Training course under the Continuing Education division. Malinda was relieved that she would not have to speak to a large audience. The idea of teaching to a small group in a classroom was a more comfortable plan. The school division posted an ad in the classified ads and in the division's curriculum schedule. Nadine, Suzanne and Cathy registered for the course and offered to help with paperwork and set up. Three people unknown to Malinda called to register. A radio station spotted the ad and asked Malinda if she would be a guest on The Ralph Koerdson Talk-Radio program. The course was starting in one week. Malinda spent most of her hours preparing. When the radio station phoned, Malinda hesitated, but having little time to think, she camouflaged the self-doubt and responded with confidence. "Yes, I would be happy to do that," she answered. The caller asked Malinda to fax the radio station with a copy of her background and list her life events on one page or less.

The night before the radio broadcast Malinda was up until 2:00 a.m. reviewing the outline of her topics on abuse and assertiveness training. She got up at 7:00 a.m. to get ready. The phone rang and when she answered, the director of the shelter home said, "The women and I are very proud of our Malinda. We are gathering together in the meeting room to listen to the radio program."

On her way to the radio station, Malinda calmed herself with a reminder that she would not have to face a large audience, at least not a visible one. When she arrived, she touched up her makeup before getting out of her car. She entered the building and a friendly receptionist greeted her and said, "I'll let Mr. Koerdson know you are here. Please have a seat. Malinda sat down and reached inside her purse for the notes she had prepared the night before. "Would you like some coffee?" the reception asked.

"No thank you," Malinda answered. Then a door opened beside the reception desk and a tall man entered the room. He was wearing a nice suit and his shoes were well polished. He looked at Malinda and said, "Follow me." She got up and walked behind him. She said "Good morning," but he did not respond. He entered another room and pointed to a chair and said, "This is where you sit; we'll be on the air in three minutes." Malinda sat at a large round table. The man sat on the opposite side facing her and said, "Make sure you speak directly into the voice box." There was a little black box with a microphone inside on the table facing her. By this time, Malinda figured out that this man was indeed *the* Ralph Koerdson and not an employee selected to escort guests to the studio. Mr. Koerdson faced a large glass window where he could see his producer on the other side. There was a red light that turned green and Mr. Koerdson began to speak. He gave a brief introduction and looked at Malinda as he asked, "Tell me, Malinda, why did you marry someone who beat you and why did you stay with him so long?" Malinda became terrified and regretted having done this but it was too late to turn back. She tried to appear calm and answered, "He's the only one that ever told me that he loved me. I stayed for ten years because in my religion it is wrong to divorce and I didn't want to be the only one in my family to fail at marriage." "How often did he beat you?" Mr. Koerdson asked. Malinda answered, "At the beginning, about once a year but each year it increased to more. He didn't need a reason to beat me. I tried really hard to figure out why."

"Would it happen when he was drunk?" asked Mr. Koerdson.

"Yes," answered Malinda.

Ralph's tone softened as he continued to ask her questions. Malinda talked about abuse and forgot all about being nervous. Then Mr. Koerdson informed his audience about the fatal crash that killed Malinda's parents and announced that another tragedy occurred when her daughter was injured in a swimming pool accident. He asked Malinda, "What effect did those traumas have on your life?" Malinda answered as though she was talking to a trusted friend. She said, "After twenty years, only recently have I been able to grieve my parents' death. Six years ago, I experienced a burnout two years after my daughter got hurt because at the same time I was facing another divorce. I thought I was going crazy so I went to my doctor for help. I was physically tired and was an emotional wreck. After Dr. Fiji ruled out mental illness, I began a journey to heal from all of this."

Every phone line lit up. He picked up the first caller. A woman that was obviously distressed spoke with a trembling voice and commended Malinda for speaking out on this subject. She began to cry as she explained how she struggled with staying out of abusive relationships. She said, "Once a relationship is over, I can't let go of the emotional pain." Another woman shared how she escaped from a violent partner and she now needed help. She said, "I finally left to save my life. But I am sad and still have demoralizing thoughts. I need to learn how to better communicate my needs." Most callers said they had difficulty with self-confidence. Others said that they kept attracting the same types of bad boys. More callers congratulated Malinda for reaching out and talking about this subject.

Mr. Koerdson stirred the pot a little more and asked Malinda in a sharp tone if her Assertive Training course would teach women how to "sock-it-to-men" and tell them off! This was a question that Malinda had anticipated and was prepared to answer. She smiled and stated that, in fact, the opposite would be taught. She explained that the Assertiveness Course would teach women how to communicate with confidence in a non-threatening manner both verbally and physically.

Mr. Koerdson announced a short three-minute break to air the radio's advertisements. Off the air Mr. Koerdson changed his demeanour and warmed up to Malinda. This time he was pleasant and made small talk. Ralph announced the program was back on the air and told his listeners about the upcoming Assertiveness Training sessions. Now callers were asking how to register for the course. Ralph gave out Malinda's phone number and thanked her for her time. When Malinda returned home, her answering machine was full and could not take any more messages. There were so many registrants that Malinda had to also rent and offer the course at a banquet room. She continued to volunteer at the shelter home.

Malinda benefited from daily relaxation exercises. She would visualize an arid desert. To represent her scrambled, worrisome thoughts, a strong gusty wind would produce a fierce sandstorm. The blowing wind and the twirling sand everywhere were an accurate representation of her troubles. The speed at which the wind blew would vary according to her state of mind. The challenge was to become calm enough that the winds quieted down and the sand would fall to the ground. The more she focused on attaining calmness, the more the chatter inside her head would quiet down. The more the winds quieted, the more the sand became still on the ground. As the winds continued to gust, her scrambled thoughts were carried away until the desert became motionless. Keeping her focus on the mental picture, Malinda stayed in that mind-set for several minutes just to enjoy the tranquility. She completed the exercise in the morning but the effects lasted long after the meditation. She noticed her day was spent with much less, if any, worry.

Convinced that the program was a healthy conditioning of the mind, she considered the routine to be just as vital as food for the nurturing of wellness. Calmness could be achieved wherever and whenever she wanted. She was becoming so proficient that the activity could be performed even while sitting in a noisy city bus. Her acquired tranquil mind became more natural to her, and worry felt unnatural.

One day Malinda followed a book's instruction to release her mind and drift to a place that would bring her the most relaxation. She counted backwards from ten to one. In a dream like state, she floated downward as she counted and arrived by a lovely stream in a plush green forest. Above her was the top of a cliff. Control could be maintained to stop the meditation at any point by counting from one to ten. She saw herself float back to the top of the cliff, back to her real life. She much preferred the picture of a boreal forest to the empty room or the dusty desert storm. But one day, her vision took a turn. While sitting in her usual chair, fully awake and enjoying the tranquility of the forest, all of sudden, sounds began to intrude into her vision. She could hear the trickling of a nearby waterfall and the cawing of a crow.

The echoes indicated that spring had arrived. A mixture of trees - majestic evergreens, white birch, and others, surrounded her. The colors of the trees and grasses were a vibrant and rich green. The sky was a deep blue. The vivid picture contained life. In her mind, Malinda's most desired childhood place of peace had returned. As the enactment continued, Malinda was drawn to rest so she curled up in a fetal position in the middle of tall wild grasses. A cool gentle breeze caressed her hair. The sun warmed her spine and the soothing warmth spread throughout her body. Malinda felt induced to close her eyes and sleep but hesitated because there could be many dangers within a woodland area. She thought to stay alert in case a bear or a pack of wolves ambushed her. These thoughts represented the scrambled worries of her mind. Like the calming of the forceful winds in the desert, Malinda responded to the forest with an instinctive awareness that below this cliff, she was completely safe from harm. Malinda felt like a little girl again, when she had been too little to realize there were actual dangers along the cow paths in the forest. This recollection of a wonderful retreat became Malinda's special scene during the meditations. It was a place where she could temporarily leave her world along with all its insecurities. The result of this particular exercise was even more astounding than any previous visualization. The aftereffects of this one produced a boost of energy that was equal to several hours of sound sleep. This relaxation stuff was turning out to be more than acquiring a calmer mindset; it was boosting her physical activity and alertness levels. Because she trusted the mental forest, Malinda allowed her mind to submit to more of its beauty. The relaxed visualization produced a doe, which was accompanied by her fawn. They both lay on a bed of flattened grass. The little one was nestled in the shelter of its mother's bosom and rested in the warmth of the sun's rays. The beauty of these two creatures amidst a perfect abode was captivating. It was like a vivid dream, a dream while Malinda was awake. In the wonder of her mind, Malinda watched the doe and fawn interact. The mother was gracious and not in the least concerned about Malinda's presence. She had a gentle look about her as though she was inviting Malinda to approach. Malinda proceeded slowly toward the pair until she stood next to the mother. She felt drawn to the little fawn and cordially asked if she could stroke the little one. The mother remained calm. She accepted Malinda and permitted her to approach even closer. Malinda advanced slowly. The doe gave a look as if to convey an invitation to lie with the two of them. Malinda was overwhelmed at the unexpected privilege. She gently sat down and was able to snuggle beside the white-speckled fawn without scaring them away. The experience was unlike any Malinda had ever known with any person or any of her favourite little farm animals. The body heat from both creatures was soothing and a sense of protection radiated from the mother's warm bosom. The fawn slept while his mother's eyes watched over him. In the absence of fear, Malinda was able to pet the little fawn. His virgin coat felt soft like fine velvet. She found security in its greatest form there.

After a while, Malinda rested her head against the mother's neck. She felt caressed against the creature's body and fell asleep. As she napped snuggled beside the fawn, the doe stayed awake and watched them sleep. The mother had entrusted Malinda with her precious offspring. The relaxation exercise had progressed into a different dimension. It was with great anticipation that Malinda took time each day to spend in the forest with her new acquaintances.

The vision continued to progress and they began to establish trust. The female deer let Malinda caress the fawn. Slowly and with a friendly approach Malinda was able to wrap both her arms around the innocent babe's silky neck. Up close, Malinda looked intently into his dark eyes, which were transparent and revealed the creature's innocence and purity. Parting from this rapture was significantly pleasant. Each good-bye resulted in a magnificent peace as she expressed gratitude with a kiss on the forehead of each animal. Malinda looked back to the peaceful visualizations during her day when doing other things, and took strength from the spiritual vision.

Divine Intervention

Richard's agreeable nature lost some of its flavour with Malinda when he would cancel plans with her to accommodate those of his mother's and grown children's. He made decisions with them without consulting her. Because he could not say no to them, Malinda was the one that he would invalidate. Malinda proposed to work out some boundaries concerning his family. Richard agreed to them, but later would ignore them. When she confronted him and explained that by saying yes to everyone, somebody was going to be let down and that that someone was always her. Richard did not disagree, nor did he agree. He simply ignored her problem. After a few months of living together, Malinda ended the relationship. Malinda bought his half of the condo and found herself living alone for the first time in her life and she became depressed.

More than ever, she relied on her relaxation exercises to help her remain grounded. One day she decided to give the meditation complete trust and released control from managing the exercise. She experienced a harmonious flow to the picturesque adventure in the usual forest visualization. She was enjoying a more peaceful mind-set when, all of a sudden, the vision took an unfavorable turn. As she counted from one to ten to bring herself back to reality, rather than floating upward she came into contact with the edge of the cliff and was clinging to its edge and clawed her way in darkness to the top of the precipice. With one hand still clinging to the edge of the cliff she grabbed some roots and hoisted herself up. Her head was level to the ground and she saw what looked like a footpath. The next thing she experienced was quite bizarre. In the vivid dream, after Malinda reached the top of the cliff, she lay on the ground fatigued from clawing her way up. She saw that the path was long and she could not see the end of it. It was very quiet and there was nothing else but perfect short grass along each side of this path. Its surface was like compressed little bits of fine clayish powder so smooth that it could be walked on barefoot. Then, out of nowhere, an opened hand reached out toward where she lay. This hand was that of a human. Malinda stretched out one of her arms and placed her hand into the palm of this hand. She was immediately pulled upright and felt a sense of peace like never before. She stood tall and straight and surprisingly came face to face with Jesus Christ. He gazed at Malinda and gently smiled. As though the encounter was real, Malinda felt affronted that religion had intruded on her relaxation vision. She spoke in a huff, "What are *you* doing here?" Her tone was unfriendly and not meant as a question. She insinuated that this figure was not invited to her personal visualizations. Christ was unmoved by her attitude and calmly answered, "You were seeking love." Malinda was speechless from hearing such a sensitive voice filled with compassion and understanding. Then the vision abruptly ended.

The visual encounter left Malinda in a state of wonderment. Although the words spoken by Christ were piercing; it was the entire expression combined with the statement that had Malinda mystified. He spoke with all of his facial features. His words came not only from his mouth but also from every part of his eyes, lips, face, mind, and emotions. The term "spoken from the heart" finally became a reality for Malinda. He looked deep into her eyes, over and beyond her attitude. Likewise, she could see beyond his words. Her rebellious nature would have hastily rebutted with a debasing statement, but she could not.

Malinda could identify the personal meanings of her visions but this one left her perplexed. When Christ appeared, she felt offended that religion intruded during the exercise but then his words melted the rebellious feeling away. Unable to interpret the visual encounter, she turned to logic. She calculated that perhaps she might have missed a portion of the explanation. She thought, *Before Christ put out his hand to help me up, maybe I had fallen or tripped on something but the road was clean and there was nothing that I could have tripped on.* The vision seemed so real that Malinda remembered every small detail of the experience. She then contemplated the symbolism of this unusual being helping her up - and from what? What was the significance of the Christ figure? Then there was the issue of receiving spoken words. This odd outcome had never happened in any previous visualization. There had been instances of hearing a brook, the wind, or birds singing. There was intuitive communication from the mother deer. All the visualizations so far were easy to interpret, but this one left Malinda in suspense. She understood nothing about this particular one. Then something came to mind. The vision contained a small but relevant detail that Malinda could not forget about. She had indeed been on a journey to find love. The incident led her to think about her childhood, when she had been confused about religion.

She remembered that a couple of years before, Hubert's wife tried to talk to her about Jesus. As their conversation turned to religion, Malinda harshly said, "Don't start that with me. I don't know that there is a God or angels or a devil or heaven and hell. All these things were taught to me without any proof or evidence that any of these exist." There was only one thing wrong with her philosophical argument. Malinda could not say the same about Jesus. He was born and lived on earth. Thousands saw him. He was a real person. He was seen, touched, and heard. She admitted, "The only thing I believe about religion is that Jesus knew how to love, and if everybody followed his example, everyone would get along with each other. He taught by backing up what he said with his actions, and that made what he said believable."

Malinda described her Christ vision to Nadine and asked if she could explain its symbolism. Much to her dismay, no explanation was provided but Nadine responded, "Why don't you come to church with me next week?" Malinda spared no thought on the subject and retorted, "No way! You know what I think about that. I've been there, done that, got the t-shirt and returned it. You know what going to church does to me. I get up on Sunday morning feeling great, I enjoy the beauty around me, and then I go to church only to come back home angry." There had been several attempts in the past to return to her childhood religion, but Malinda decided she was going to stop repeating what was offensive in her life and religion was one of those things. She could not accept that women were excluded from becoming priests nor would she yield to condescending sermons about divorce. Malinda found these particular issues demeaning to women. At the same time, she felt guilty for having those views; that is, until one day when she freed herself from the tortures of her fight between blame and responsibility.

Malinda explained to Nadine how she didn't want to spin that cycle once again. "You know how much I tried to conform to religion and that I finally laid it to rest and put closure to it." Nadine inherited some of her mother's persistence and continued to nudge Malinda. She said, "My church is not like the one you went to." Malinda answered, "I'll repeat, each time I go to church I come out of it angry. I'm not doing that again!" Nadine also knew her mother well. She explained how her wheelchair could not go to where her friends sat in church so she had to sit alone. Malinda asked, "Can't they sit with you?" Nadine answered, "No, mom. They sit in a section assigned for the youth ministry and it is not wheelchair accessible." Then she added, "I have to sit alone in an aisle where I am noticed by everyone." Malinda could not bear the thought of her daughter being ostracized from her friends and left to sit alone because of her wheelchair. "Okay, I'll go just so you don't have to sit alone."

Nadine was appreciative and suggested that each Sunday after church they could go for lunch at the mall and call it their mother-daughter outing. The first Sunday they arrived at church, Malinda was surprised that the service was in a banquet hall, which the church rented on Sundays. The setting was completely different from what she knew church to be. There were no altars, pews or heavenly icons. Hundreds of chairs were organized as though a seminar was about to take place. There were electric guitars, keyboards, and a full set of drums on the stage. Malinda had gone to a wedding social in the same auditorium about a year prior. She thought, *this is no church!*

Nadine led the way and Malinda followed. "We'll sit here, mom. My chair won't block the aisle here," Several people, young and old alike, came to greet Nadine. They sat behind a friendly lady who was also in a wheelchair. A handful of well-groomed musicians climbed onto the stage and took their positions at their instruments. Behind them followed the choir. Three lead singers stood at the front behind their microphones and stands. A choir conductor stepped out and faced the choir. The music began. The congregation stood up. The first number sounded like rock 'n roll with electric guitars screeching and drums pounding heavily to the beat of a contemporary Christian song. People clapped hands and some moved their bodies in rhythm with the music. There were two large screens on each side of the stage that showed the lyrics for sing along. Malinda whispered to Nadine, "What is this, a concert?" Nadine was reading the pamphlet that the greeters gave at the door. She looked at her mother and smiled. Malinda asked, "How many people are here?" Nadine answered, "Over a thousand and there's about one thousand more coming tonight for the evening service."

During the fourth song, a tall, dark and handsome man walked from the center front row onto the stage. He sang the fourth and last song with the crowd. When the number finished, the music group cleared the stage and the handsome man was brought a fancy podium made of thick Plexiglas. Things got quiet for a moment when the man began to pray out loud. He asked God to lead the service and his words that he was about to preach. Then he introduced himself as Pastor Leo. Malinda thought, *alright; no altar, no pews, no statues, no robes and the pastor is wearing a suit. This will only last an hour and then we can go out for lunch.*

The pastor sounded more like a motivational speaker than a member of the clergy. He definitely had charisma. Pastor Leo captivated and maintained Malinda's attention when he explained each point of the topic entitled, Seven Keys to Leadership. He used the example of Moses in the Bible when he led a million slaves out of Egypt. The pastor had the ability to describe the event in detail and brought the story to life with the issues that Moses had and compared it with modern times. She found the topic sensible and realistic. Moreover, it directly related to her course studies. On the following Sunday Malinda brought her notebook and pencil to take notes. The opening musical numbers were soothing that day. While Malinda stood along with the crowd, she closed her eyes and used the music to meditate. Soon the singing sounded like it came from afar and Malinda was swept away into her place of inner peace. That Sunday, Pastor Leo spoke about managing emotions and how to discipline impulses and achieve self-control, topics that deeply interested her. As the weeks went by, Malinda gathered numerous pages of notes.

Un-Changing

A particular man in the congregation sat near Malinda whenever he could. He was bald and had protruding ears. He had a hefty build and was well dressed. One Sunday he sat across the aisle from her. Malinda looked his way as he was looking her way. He smiled and she smiled back. He always sat alone and Malinda noticed that he wore no wedding ring. The following Sunday, he sat directly behind her. When the service was over, he introduced himself as Greg and made small talk with Malinda and Nadine. He asked if Malinda would meet him for coffee one night during the week. She answered, "Possibly, yes." She noticed his striking smile and full lips. He asked for her phone number and she gave it to him. He thanked her and said, "I'll call you."

After a few weeks Greg and Malinda saw each other on a regular basis. Each Sunday Greg sat next to Malinda in church. One Sunday he did not. Malinda looked for him among the crowd when she saw him with two children. She went up to them and Greg introduced the children as his own and Malinda as one of daddy's friends. After the service, Greg was nowhere to be found. Later that week, he phoned at the last minute to break a dinner date. She forced herself to do something she enjoyed instead of wallowing in self-pity alone at home. She went to the mall where her favorite pet shop had always soothed away any loneliness when she held little rabbits and hamsters. That particular evening the furry little creatures failed to fill the emptiness. She was walking out of the mall when she saw Greg and his two children walk in. Malinda was happy to see them and hoped she might spend some time with them. She walked up to them and said, "Hi!" Greg nodded his head and continued to walk past Malinda. On her way home she recalled when Greg had told her that she was special to him. Clearly, his reaction relayed the opposite message. Malinda made up her mind to break up the affair. She cried so much she had a hard time seeing while she drove home. An old familiar pain in the pit of her stomach came back.

When she arrived home Malinda retaliated with anger. She phoned Greg and yelled, "How can you not even stop and talk to me?" Greg began to speak, but Malinda didn't let him and accused him of treating her like some distant acquaintance. "I never want to see you again," she shouted, and then hung up on him.

The after-effects of this breakup were not nearly as devastating as her other ones. Malinda was emotionally and cognitively better at handling the end of a relationship. Pastor Leo's sermons about how to stay focused echoed and she could no longer ignore that while she pursued the affections of a man, she neglected her own future plans.

To regain direction in her life, Malinda went to see her counselor. During the appointment the counselor suggested to use what worked for her to get grounded –meditation. Her counselor added, "But before, ask for wisdom." The next morning, Malinda closed her eyes and enter the relaxed state. Something amazing occurred. A precise statement came to mind. ***We have our spirit from birth and as we approval seek, we separate from our spirit until we re-connect again.***

Malinda learned and taught this insight as it developed. As she worked out the concept of having a spirit she sought to be able to explain it. She gave the insight the benefit of the doubt and concluded that her approval seeking caused her to separate from her spirit which she compared to the loss of her authenticity. But it was not so easy to understand reconnection to the spirit. She thought, *I changed for others to like me. Now, for me to re-connect with my spirit, I need to un-change.* As she worked the idea out she used it to explain to the women at the shelter home that she was not trying to get them to change but to un-change. When she introduced the topic some of the women frowned and argued that it was impossible to do that. One of them said, "You can't change the past." Malinda explained that as a battered wife, she stayed stuck in the mud because she changed in order to please others, either her husband, her friends or her family members, or all of the above. She said, "I was like a chameleon. Changing to suit the situation or person and become what I thought they wanted me to be like. I got drunk when I really didn't want to. I was a doormat but I wanted to be confident. I'd say nothing when I wanted to say no." The women's frowns turned to nodding and verbal agreement. They could always relate to Malinda's own life experience. Malinda continued the lesson, adding, "I changed for other people. Approval from another person gave me a feeling that I was accepted or wanted. To please my husband I did what he wanted me to do, no matter what. It cost me plenty. I traded in my values in order to be loved. I put my self aside to fill his need but in the end all I got back was hurt. I lost so much even my identity. After my second divorce, I asked, "What am I?" And the answer was that I was something and not someone. I was a secretary, mother, auntie, sister, daughter-in-law and a volunteer worker. I was connected with all that I did, but not with *who* I was. I disconnected from my heart, my moral fiber, which I now recognize to be my spirit, the core of who I am. I dig deep and peel away the layers of lies, hurt and deceit, even from myself. The process of un-changing brought me closer and closer to my real identity. I no longer want to change who I am in order to please someone. My journey is one of re-discovering who and what I really am. I got tired of trying to get somebody to give me what he or she could not, would not and did not have. Like a chameleon, forever changing in order to blend in. The years spent seeking approval from others was driven by an unrelenting urge to be accepted and recognized.

To re-discover my authentic self, I had to journey into my own soul. Although I left the dysfunctional upbringing of my childhood, I carried its model wherever I went. Malinda asked, "How do we undo change and re-connect with self?" The women answered, "By un-changing!" The room filled with laughter and excitement as the women exclaimed over this new approach. They didn't have to change; they had to un-change.

Return of a Friend

One of Malinda's former property rental clients named Garth tracked her down and left a message on her phone to call him. Because Garth was illiterate, Malinda used to spend more time with him to explain the contents of his contract agreements. Appointments with him used to last well over an hour; at times their visit wasn't all about business. The two often shared their similar childhood memories over a cup of coffee, which was when they discovered that their backgrounds were quite similar, except for the fact that Garth's family was very poor.

When Malinda returned Garth's call, he explained that he wanted to talk to her about something and offered to buy her a drink at a certain hotel. Malinda answered, "I don't go to bars any more." Garth said, "Okay then, I'll buy you dinner. You pick the place." A couple of days later, they met at a restaurant. Garth was a man who always cut to the chase. As soon as Malinda arrived, she sat down and immediately Garth explained that he was having problems with one of his tenants. "Hello Garth," said Malinda. "You still look the same as you did ten years ago." Garth was a tall and husky man with black curly hair and brown eyes. The waiter came to their table and asked what they wanted to drink. Malinda ordered a red wine and Garth ordered a coffee. "It's good to see an old friend," added Malinda. "Yes, it's good to see you, too." said Garth. "I want to pay you to take over the affairs of my property with the bad tenant," he added. Malinda said, "I am no longer working in that field since my divorce with Gerry." Garth said, "I found that out when I contacted the company." Garth was not about to give up. He was not about to take no for an answer as he commented, "I want you to manage just one property. The tenant is not paying his rent and I don't know how to take legal action to correct the problem." Malinda suggested that there were several companies in the city that would do that for him but Garth insisted again, "but I want you to do it!" Malinda said, "I'm really not interested in going back to the old job." Why don't you want to hire a company?" she asked. Garth answered, "Because my reading is limited. I trust you. I've been burnt too often by those who take advantage of me because I cannot read." Malinda thought for a moment and said, "One property won't take up too much of my time." The waiter returned with their drinks and dropped off two menus. "Will you do it?" asked Garth. Malinda answered, "For an old friend, I'll do just the one property." Garth was happy and thanked her. He added, "We'll discuss the rest of the details later. First, I am curious about what you said on the phone, that you don't go to bars any more." Malinda answered, "Since my divorce I made some lifestyle changes. I don't drink alcohol any more other than an occasional glass of wine with dinner." Garth commented, "I am glad for you. I don't like bars either." Malinda asked, "Why did you ask to take me to one?" "Oh, I just wanted to accommodate you. What other changes have you made?" She told him about changing her career goals to become a counselor and public speaker. She added that she was gaining experience while working in a shelter home for women. They talked about where they were now living but Garth asked again if there were any other changes in her life. Malinda answered, "There is one, but I'm not sure you want to hear about it." "Well, that makes me even more curious. What is it?" he persisted. Malinda knew he would be relentless until she told him. She began to tell him that something was on her mind lately and explained how she had adopted relaxation exercises to help calm her nerves. She continued, "I only told my one daughter but it would be nice to get this off my chest. Something unusual happened. I had a vision." The waiter returned and took their order. Garth couldn't wait to put down the menu. After the waiter left, he asked, "What kind of vision?" Malinda became quiet. She lowered her head then looked up at Garth. She studied his expression and could see caring and sincerity in his eyes. She concluded that Garth was the right person to tell. A further benefit was that he did not keep company with any of her family or former friends. She told him every detail of the Christ vision. Garth often interrupted Malinda while she talked but not this time. He listened attentively to every word she said. Their meals came and Garth stated, "I want to talk more about this."

After dinner they made arrangements to meet the next day and view Garth's rental property.

It was 10:00 a.m. when Garth showed up. They went to his favorite coffee shop where they took care of the paperwork and finalized their work agreement. Then Garth said, "I hope you're not in a hurry to get back because I want to continue the talk we had yesterday." Malinda answered, "Sure, I have an hour." He said, "Many years ago I had a vision of owning a property where people went to get to know God and to heal from bad things that happened when they were kids." Malinda listened attentively. Then Garth confided that when he was growing up, his mother used to beat him almost every week. He added, "She told me every day that I was no good for nothing. She would take me outside where my dad chopped wood, pick up a piece of split wood and hit me several times across the spine with the sharp edge." Garth took a sip of coffee, and then added; "Now that's painful." Then there came a surprise. He proposed an idea. He said, "If my tenants don't pay their rent, you'll have to kick them out. If that happens, why don't you rent the place and have some of your clients live in it and you could counsel people and run healing courses." Garth then said something Malinda never expected to hear him say. "You know, that vision you had was from God," he announced. Malinda answered, "I know." Garth asked, "How do you know?" Malinda explained that after her vision, she went to church with her daughter and that she started to read the Bible. Garth never spoke about God in the many years that she had known him. Garth said, "I love to talk about God." Malinda was surprised to hear him say that. She asked, "How long have you been religious?" He said, "I'm not religious, I was born-again at the age of nineteen." Then he asked, "Are you born-again?" Malinda asked, "What does that mean, born again?" Instead of explaining the meaning, Garth asked her a series of other questions. "Do you want to know God?" She answered, "Yeah, of course." Then he asked, "Why?" Malinda thought for a moment and answered, "Well, when I decided that I didn't want to repeat the same mistakes over and over again and stopped blaming my dad and husbands for my divorces, I realized that there must be something wrong with me. And so I began to look at myself in order to heal my emotional damage. I read several books on abuse and how to recover from it." Malinda continued to tell about how she began to practice relaxation exercises. "Sometimes when I reach complete peace, with my eyes closed, I can see the purest light which looks like one that I saw one night, long ago, when I was rescued from being killed by Brian; except this light is closer and brighter but it never hurts my eyes. In the visions, sometimes I look at it and other times, I stand in it," Then she affirmed, "I think that's God." Garth said, "So, you want to be a better person?" Malinda replied, "That's another way of putting it." Garth quickly asked, "Do you know Jesus?" This time, Malinda did not have to think about it and answered just as quickly, "Jesus did exist and he showed us how to love." She paused for a moment and said, "You must think that I've gone loco." She expected Garth to tell her to get some help but his reaction was quite the opposite. He was all ears and asked, "Do you think I'm nuts?" Malinda replied, "Not at all!" "I told you that I like to talk about God," he said. Then he asked if she experienced anything else about God. Malinda felt more at ease and said, "Oh, yes! Just last week, in church while I was listening to the music and songs that were being played, I was standing like everyone else, only I closed my eyes and got into my place of peace inside myself when I saw Jesus again. He stood really close to me. His face almost touched mine. I know I was smiling. Then, during this occurrence, in my mind, I said, "Hello." Then Jesus did something totally unexpected and began to dance by himself down the church aisle. I thought at the time, this couldn't be Jesus. He doesn't dance! It happened again on a different Sunday. I noticed the way he danced. He was graceful and elegant. With each motion of his arms, it made his loose garment sway with the rhythm of the music. Then I remembered that possibly Jesus could have danced. He went to weddings. At one wedding, he turned water into wine. Of course Jesus danced!" Garth commented, "Your excitement is making you glow as if that bright light is shining on you right now." Malinda giggled and said, "I should get going." The two left the café and agreed to meet again at the same place in a week from that day.

White Teeth for the Calling

From the rekindling of that past relationship, Malinda had someone with whom to share her encounters with Christ. Garth seemed to understand but during another visit, he continued to run Malinda through the mill and asked, "Do you believe God can heal all kinds of diseases?" The reply from his subject beginner was an immediate, "Yes." Testing her further he asked, "Do you believe God can grow a limb, like a bone?" "Yes, I believe God can do that," Malinda answered. Garth was silent for a moment before he told her about times when he witnessed such events. He told her about a healing service in the United States where he saw a man in a wheelchair grow a shorter leg to become the same length as his other. "I saw that with my own eyes," he affirmed. He went on and told about many other unusual healings he had witnessed. Then, his attitude changed and he asked, "Do you believe God can remove fillings and make a person's teeth all white again?" Malinda said, "I don't see why not. If he can grow bones he can do that!" Garth replied with a profound voice and said, "No," and continued to say, "At those meetings, people asked for white teeth and it didn't happen. After the healing service they still had lead fillings in their mouth." That statement confused Malinda. She trusted everything Garth had told her because, in her view, he had memorized most of the Bible by listening to taped recordings while she was only entertaining the possibility of the Christ in her visions and was thinking about that means for tremendous healing. She asked Garth to tell her more about the wonderful things he had seen God do but instead, he replied, "You are born-again." He asked her a final question. "What are you going to do?" Malinda took a deep breath and replied, "Before the relaxing exercises, I ventured to try something new. I wanted more than to cure my anxiety and finger twitching. I wanted more than to develop the skill of relaxation. I was after answers. I read book upon book about how to live in a more meaningful way. I found a place within myself where it is like entering into a bubble but it's more like a state of mind when there is a connection with my entire body and, I think, my soul. It's where I have immeasurable peace. Before that peace, I would see a light and feel privileged to be able to bask in it. The result was gratitude for having been the recipient of such a miracle, a peace I have never experienced in my entire life thus far. Sometimes I saw a mental image of my body wrapped in a white satin, fluffy blanket that provided warmth and security. Each time this happened, I would see the light change into a green colour. I thought this must be what it feels like to be inside a cocoon, which is wrapped with a green leaf while a caterpillar undergoes its transformation. It was like healing was happening but I didn't know what from. And that was not the last of my spiritual encounters in the relaxation visions I explored. There was one that gave me a picture of something different. There appeared four separate and significant words written in bold, capitalized letters. This is what I saw." Malinda wrote on a piece of paper the words, HEAL TEACH PREACH LEAD, and showed it to Garth. She continued to say, "That is what I saw and I knew it was a direction to what I am supposed to do. I was already counseling but to teach was something I had struggled about, thinking that it meant I would have to get a Bachelor of Education degree. The groups I was facilitating made me realize that I was already teaching. I had been facilitating groups and telling them about my life experience and my recovery methods at universities and schools in a continuing education capacity. Now, to preach is something I cannot do. It is far too large a leap to take on such a task. Why, to preach about God is far too unrelated to my course material. I want to be a public speaker, but not a preacher."

Garth understood everything she told him and thought he could understand what she was going through. She was hoping he would agree but instead, he said that he was also called to preach some seventeen years ago and still hadn't taken the step. Malinda commented, "Garth, for you, I can see that happening. You have the gift of memory. Even if I listen to twice the audio you have on the Bible, I still couldn't memorize more than three sentences." She continued to say, "I have been listening to your life experiences and I can tell you that you have a unique gift of being able to narrate one of your painful events and even add humour to it. As for me, what kind of preacher cannot memorize Bible verses? God has surely tapped the wrong person on the shoulder. Anyway, Churches would not accept a twice-divorced woman preacher. It's a ridiculous idea."

Garth returned to his home in the north of the province and said he would not be back for at least three months. A few weeks later, during a church service she attended with her daughter, Malinda heard there was a female guest who was going to perform a healing service at the church. Malinda attended only to observe what a preacher woman would be like. The auditorium was filled with people. The guest speaker told about all kinds of miraculous healings she had seen. The woman preacher didn't speak any different than a male speaker. She was normal and the talk was nothing new to Malinda until she said, "Some people have prayed for white teeth and they received white teeth."

The speaker's statement about white teeth brought Malinda to attention. She thought, "Well, if God gave white teeth to some people, then He could give me some." But Garth said this couldn't happen so Malinda doubted that it would. At that moment, Malinda prayed to God. In silence she conveyed, "Yeah, I want white teeth. That would be really nice. I always wanted white teeth like the movie actresses have. I would have a nice white smile." After relaying this wish, she stopped and remembered that Pastor Leo said that when you ask God for something that your desire had to align with God's will. Malinda pondered shortly how her request could be God's will and not just her vanity. As her heart doubted that it would even happen, she asked anyway and got the idea to use the occasion as a way out of the calling to preach. Then she changed her request and prayed, "God, you want me to preach and I would look more appealing with white teeth in my mouth when I speak." Then she had a second thought that if her teeth did become all white, then she would have to preach. On her way home she looked in the visor mirror with her mouth wide open and saw that the lead fillings were all still intact. When she arrived home she went straight to the bathroom mirror and did the same thing. Nothing had changed. Malinda smiled. Then, she noticed that something *was* different. She moved closer to the mirror. Her smile seemed brighter. Her front teeth seemed whiter. Only thing, those teeth never had fillings to begin with. She asked God, "How come my front teeth look whiter?" But no answer came. *Oh, I get it*, she thought, *it's my attitude that's different. It's part of my low self- esteem recovery. My front teeth aren't as yellow as I perceived them to be. You changed my destructive belief about having unattractive teeth.* Malinda began to pray, "Thank you God, You have made a miracle. You changed my attitude about my teeth. Never again will I think I have ugly teeth. They are nice looking teeth. I had a nice smile all along." From that day on, Malinda thought her smile was beautiful even with the many grey fillings in all her back teeth, and she was thankful that she still had her own teeth.

Five weeks later, in September, Malinda received a phone call from Richard. It had been nearly a year since they last spoke. At first he just made idle chitchat. Immediately Malinda thought he was going to ask her out. As she prepared to kindly turn him down, he asked, "Did you recently receive a cheque in the mail from my insurance company?" Malinda answered, "No, nothing came for you in the mail."

"I mean a cheque sent to *you*, in *your* name," he clarified. Malinda answered, "After we separated I closed my investment account with your company and they paid me a bit of interest." Richard asked, "How much did they charge you in withdrawal fees?" Malinda became apprehensive and answered, "I don't remember exactly how much, but I did lose some money for cashing the investment prematurely. Why are you asking?" Richard replied, "Because you're getting that money back. The company still has you named as my common-law wife, which means that you are entitled to benefits. You will receive a refund cheque in the mail." Malinda was taken aback by his integrity and exclaimed, "Boy! That is good news." Then Richard added, "There's also my dental plan and you are still entitled to benefits. Your dental work is still covered plus you can be reimbursed for any dental bills you paid for since the split up." Malinda doodled on a piece of note paper and wrote some of the things Richard told her as he continued to explain, "Just submit copies of receipts paid to your dentist and mail them to the insurance company for a full refund." Malinda exclaimed, "Wow, I can't believe this! I had a root canal done. Will they pay me back for that? It was over

$600.00, you know." Richard answered, "Yes, plus, any dental work you need done for the rest of this year until your benefits terminate on December 31." Malinda softened her voice and with humbleness said, "Thank you, Richard. This is very good news."

Shortly after Richard's call, Malinda became doubtful that the supposed reimbursements would happen. A week later an envelope arrived in the mail erasing all her doubts. She opened the mail and found nine cheques each representing reimbursements for the penalty charges she paid for when closing her fund investments. Malinda arranged each cheque in a row on her kitchen counter. She gazed at them for a while, then got her palm calculator and added them up. When she hit the equal button, the digital display showed a total of $1,112.73. She gathered the cheques and made them ready for a bank deposit. She wasted no time in submitting her former dental receipts for a refund. Two weeks later, another cheque was received in the amount of $900.00. Malinda phoned the dentist and made an appointment to have her teeth cleaned – a procedure that was long overdue.

In the dentist's office, Malinda sat in the big reclining chair, happy that the cost for that appointment was covered under Richard's medical plan. After the dental hygienist finished with the regular procedure, the dentist entered the room. He checked the condition of Malinda's teeth. He commented that one tooth had a sizeable lead filling. He said, "This tooth is almost all filling; so much that the grey shows on the exterior. It is the fourth tooth from the front." He handed Malinda a mirror. She saw how that one tooth next to the freshly cleaned teeth was grey from its sizeable filling. The dentist told her he could replace the old lead filling and insert a white filling in its stead. The dentist further commented, "You would have a nice white smile." Because of cost, Malinda hesitated to approve the work. As though the dentist had read her mind, he next stated that the insurance company would cover the cost because the old lead filling was due to be redone. "I'll let you think about it and I'll be back in a couple of minutes."

Malinda reclined comfortably in the big chair with her feet up and thought, *It would be desirable to have a nice white smile while teaching, especially if I'm to have a career in public speaking.* Then it hit her… *This is exactly what I had asked for*, she thought, and remembered how she had asked God to give her white teeth.

Her dentist had spoken the exact words that she used during her prayer request.

When the dentist returned, Malinda challenged God and asked if the dental plan would cover the cost of replacing all her grey fillings for she had many of them. He inspected her teeth once again and said, "It would cover all the lead fillings that were done more than five years ago. Since that is the case with your fillings, yes, the cost would be covered." By the end of that year, all of Malinda's teeth were white. In spring the following year, Garth paid her a visit. When Malinda showed him that God gave her all white teeth and explained how it happened, Garth had nothing to say.

As a result of her white teeth experience, Malinda felt she knew God a little more. She got more than what she asked for. Her self-image had improved; her financial picture had improved; and lastly, she had received all white teeth. In her own understanding, Malinda learned that the miracle was not instantaneous at the moment she prayed for it, but over a short period of time it had been accomplished through Richard and her dentist. She understood that miracles don't always happen instantly and how and when they occurred was up to God. She came to trust in Him, that when she prayed for something, she could have the reassurance that God would provide. Her prayers from then on began with confidence that she would receive, and so she gave thanks. Whenever she asked, she left the how and the when up to God.

A Valentine Love Note

With her continued attendance at church with Pastor Leo, she healed a lot, but there was still some pain. One Sunday morning she saw Greg and his children walk in and immediately thought about how they met in church and how he had treated her. His presence reactivated old anger, bitterness, sorrow and pain. The choir began to sing. Malinda stood up with the rest of the congregation and closed her eyes to enjoy the music. Immediately, her father came to mind. That familiar cold and empty place within her echoed how she had never been special to anyone. She became so weary of the relentless pain the thoughts about her father produced. She tried to hold back tears and thought, *If only he could have made me feel special, my life would have been so much better.* She contemplated on how her father had been so emotionally and physically cold towards her. She thought about what she had always wanted to say to him. In her mind, she could boldly ask the ultimate question as though she were speaking to her live dad. *How come you never made me feel special?* Her question was barely finished when an answer quickened from her spirit, how *could I make you feel special when I don't know what that is like?* A familiar cliché came to mind, you *can't give what you don't have.* For the first time, a common cliché made her understand that her father could not make her feel special because *he* never felt special himself. She realized how she would understand and could forgive others for the same imperfection, but not her father. Time after time she held him at fault for any lover's lack of caring.

Pastor Leo came to the pulpit and the congregation sat down. Malinda opened her eyes and sat also. She took out her notepad and wrote what she had just experienced. When she finished she felt overwhelming compassion and love. Her writing continued to flow and she wrote the following love note. *I forgive you, dad. I'm* *sorry you were never made to feel special by the people you loved. You <u>are</u> special. You always were. I saw it in you and I wanted you to give me some. It's not that you didn't have it. It's that you didn't know you had it. I love you and you are special."*

Still captivated by the experience, she reached the end of the writing when she realized it was Valentine's Day. She ended the note by writing, *today, father, on this Valentine's Day, I LOVE YOU.* Instead of being the recipient of the kind words she so desperately wanted to hear from her father, from a place deep within her spirit, the opposite happened, and Malinda gave rather than received. She became the giver of the very thing she wanted to receive; however, that day, she got something far greater. She understood that if her father could have expressed his emotions openly to her that those words were what he would have said. From that moment on, the need to feel special by her dad vanished and never returned again. Her perception about her dad made a turn around and she loved him unconditionally.

Have Your Own

During a meditation, Malinda asked for direction as to where to apply for a job. She received the impression *Have your own.* Being the proprietor of a business was something she vowed never to do again. There were too many responsibilities, not to mention the financial risk involved. She never forgot the stresses of running a business during her partnership with Gerry. She put the idea out of her mind. Her condo and car were both paid for. She had enough money left in her bank account to carry her through the next few months. *By then*, she thought, *I'll have a job.* After all, she was just looking for part time work. With her car and condo paid for, along with a part time job, there would be time and money for a yearly vacation in the south each year. If a job in the field of her studies did not materialize, she planned to use her years of experience in financial management and her future would be secure.

After a couple of months the money in the bank was steadily decreasing. Plan B was something she diligently avoided. It made her stomach literally sick to think about going back to her old job. Before meditation one afternoon, she asked to see what *her own* would look like and what it would be called. With her eyes closed, she began to see letters slowly descending from a deep blue space on high. The first letter to appear was an S followed by E, R, E and N. Malinda assumed that the word spelled Serene. She thought how it would be a great name for an emotional healing center. But more letters continued to flow and formed the word SERENITY. She asked, "Serenity what?" No more letters appeared. The vision ended.

A few days later, Garth phoned. He was in a panic and said that his tenants had moved out without notice. "Can I meet with you?" he exclaimed. Can you be ready in half an hour?" Malinda agreed. Garth picked her up and drove a couple of miles past the city limits to a beautifully landscaped acreage with a large bungalow and an oversized attached garage. The house had three bedrooms on the main floor. One of them was a large master bedroom with an ensuite bathroom and walk-in closet. The rest of the two thousand square foot area consisted of a den and living room, each with a wood burning fireplace made of graphite rock that reached all the way up to the ceiling. The kitchen had fine pine cupboards with brass hinges. The cozy dining room that opened to the sunken living room added flair and charm to the design. The main floor was complete with a five-piece bathroom. The basement was completely finished with an eight hundred square foot recreational room with a wood burning stove, another bathroom and two more bedrooms. The property was loaded with country charm and country flair. The house looked more like a villa or a lodge. Afterwards Garth and Malinda went to their favourite coffee shop. Malinda asked, "Have you considered selling your property rather than hiring me to manage it?" Garth shook his head. "I'll tell you why. God wants me to build a Christian center – a place where people can come to heal from the bad things that happened to them in the past." Garth began to draw on a restaurant serviette and said, "This is what I saw in a vision from God." He drew two buildings. One was a chapel and the other was a residence. Malinda commented, "Well, you already have the residence. When are you planning to build the chapel?" "I don't know," Garth replied. Malinda asked, "How long ago did you receive this vision?" Garth answered, "Seventeen years ago." "What are you waiting for?" asked Malinda. "I am waiting until I am finished working up north and I can move back to the city." "How long do you think that will take?" continued Malinda. He answered, "I don't know. I am making a lot of money up there." Malinda finalized the management agreement and settled a fee for service for managing the property.

Later that evening Garth called and said he had an idea. He was headed back up north the next day and asked to meet right away. Garth was waiting for Malinda at the coffee shop. "What's on your mind?" asked Malinda. Garth answered, "After we talked yesterday, I got an idea." "I'm listening," said Malinda. "Why don't you rent the property and counsel people there instead of working from your home?" "Why, I am not ready for something like that. I don't want to own my own center. It's much too much hassle and anyway, I can't afford the rent." The rent Garth wanted was expensive and did not include heat and electricity. Garth would not leave without a go ahead for his plan. He added, "Well, you could charge rent and have some residents stay that need refuge from the world while you help them. You could run a healing program here." Malinda quickly rejected the proposition, but her own vision of the word Serenity lit up in her mind and remained fixed there - even while they talked. She hoped that Garth would offer to help fund the project. *After all*, she thought, *it's his idea and he can afford it.* Testing the waters, she asked, "If I was to consider this plan, would you partner with me?" "Well, of course," Garth answered. "I'll be back in six months. I could arrange to stay longer and help you out during my stopover." Malinda knew that Garth would be stubborn about activating this idea of his and he would not take no for an answer. "I'll think about it," said Malinda. "I'll see you in six months," she concluded. Garth paid for the coffees and headed outside. Malinda followed him to a new truck. She asked "Hey, is that red truck yours?" "Yeah, answered Garth. "I came into town to buy it. I'll call you in a couple of days." He drove away in a shiny red pickup truck.

The next day Malinda prepared an ad to post the property in a newspaper classified rentals section. While she prepared the write-up, a whisper, *have your own*, set in her mind. When she finished the ad, she left the paper sitting on her desk and postponed her phone call to the newspaper while she went jogging. When she returned, she lay comfortably on the living room floor to do her daily relaxation exercise. In her mind, she surrendered all expectations and requested only to be in a place of peace. The white light appeared. She enjoyed the quiet of the moment when she began to see a vision of Garth's property. There were people walking about the back yard and she saw herself in the house preparing an outline for a course she was about to facilitate.

That evening, Garth phoned her. "Did you think about my idea?" he asked. Malinda evaded the question. "I thought you'd call tomorrow," she replied. "I got in early. So, are you going to run your program at my property?" Malinda planned to say that it's too risky but instead, she answered, "The place will be called Serenity House."

Malinda threw away the rental ad she had prepared for Garth's property and wrote up her own condo for rent instead. She listed it as a furnished unit in the classified ads. Her place rented immediately. She packed up her personal belongings and moved into Serenity House. Three of her clients moved in to undergo a Christian faith healing program. One of the residents was a woman in her early twenties named Roberta who was going through a burnout with depression. Another was a forty-two year old man, Peter, who was seeking help for alcoholism and depression. He loved yard work and was happiest when riding on the mowing tractor. He would keep the grounds looking like a park. The third resident was a man who had drifted in from Quebec and had just left his wife and children. He claimed he would be helpful to Malinda by giving his time as her helper.

Addiction rehabilitation and counseling centres began to refer more clients to Serenity House. Malinda ran workshops named "How to Emotionally Survive Abuse" and "Christian-based Twelve Step Addiction Recovery." Outside participants joined residents to attend weekly sessions. They came with their different problems, but had one request in common, how to connect with God. Malinda complied with their request and added another course she named "Divine Guidance", DG for short.

The White Stone

A grand opening was planned. Word got around and a radio station contacted Serenity House to broadcast the event. A television station also called to interview her and the volunteers for the evening news. The morning of the celebration was a busy one. Malinda began with organizing the house, giving each resident a few chores to do. They were excited about this special day and were happy to help. Hubert and Cathy came to help. They swept the floor of the attached garage and made it into a small hall. Malinda placed a music stand in a corner with a flip chart beside it. This was Malinda's first time to preach about God to a public audience.

It was two hours before people would start to arrive. Peter was on the riding mower doing some last minute yard grooming. Malinda was nervous and decided to go for a short jog to ease tension and stop in a secluded area to get some inspiration for her lecture.

She walked at a fast pace down the driveway when she noticed a piece of paper next to a barb wire fence. The yard should have no littering, especially today. Peter will pick it up. Then, an inner voice said to pick it up. Malinda thought, it's not my job; it's Peter's. Again the inner voice repeated to pick it up. Malinda felt it was DG speaking to her so she did. She walked to the fence and bent down to pick up the paper when she saw another paper a few feet away. She walked over to pick that one up when she found beside it a nice white stone. It was the size of her hand. She loved to collect unique stones as a child and she couldn't resist that one. It was well driven into the ground and she couldn't dig it up. She removed the dirt around it to loosen it. Peter yelled, "What did you find?" "It's just a rock," Peter came running over. It was unusual for him to pay attention to what Malinda was doing. When he got near Malinda, he became excited. "That's a real nice rock. Do you want me to dig it out?" Malinda answered, "Yeah. I have to go jogging." Malinda headed down the road running while Peter got a shovel to dig around the rock. Later when Malinda returned, Peter said, "Come look at your find. I washed it." Peter led Malinda into the garage where the meeting was to be held. In the middle of the floor was more than a little rock. It was a beautiful white marbled rock. Peter said, "It weighs nearly 70 pounds. I put it in the middle of the floor to use as a centre piece for our gathering."

Malinda wasn't pleased about that. She answered, "We will not do that. The centre of attention today is Jesus the Christ. You may put it in a corner somewhere." Peter did as he was told. Malinda wrote the words she received earlier during her jogging. Love never dies. She set up a microphone and stand; then placed 30 chairs in a circle from one side of her podium to the next.

First to arrive at the grand opening were the radio and TV crews. They interviewed the residents as well as the volunteers, Hubert and Cathy. Soon after, forty people arrived including Malinda's two daughters. A group of four women came to Malinda and introduced themselves as Peter's friends. One of them noticed the white stone and asked, "Where does that rock come from?" Malinda answered, "I found it this morning on the property line. Peter dug it out for me."

"Do you know what kind of stone that is?"

"No," said Malinda.

"It's quartz – not common in this part of the country. It's mainly found up north."

Malinda commented, "Well, Garth, the owner of the property, probably brought it here from where he works up north. How do you know what type of rock it is?"

"My dad owns a quarry in the southeast of the province. I worked with him from the time I was ten until he sold it when I was twenty-one. He taught me about various types of stones. You have an unusual piece. We should take it out of the corner and put it in front for the people to get its energy."

Malinda was perturbed but simply answered, "Christ is the center of attention today."

Garth surprised Malinda with his arrival. He walked up to the front and told someone to get a bar stool from the basement. He had his guitar with him and strapped it over one of his shoulders. He struck a few chords and said, "That will do."

"I'll sing a few songs," he announced on the mike. It was the first time Malinda heard him sing. She was quite pleased. Then, everyone sat down.

Malinda spoke about her latest messages received from DG. She really didn't know what would follow, then a leading of Divine Spirit guided her to tell the people to stand and form a circle. Malinda walked over to the CD player and held her finger on the pause button. Everybody was in the circle - even the two media crews. Malinda told the group to just be quiet and spend a couple of minutes in serenity with Christ. The music started and Malinda stood beside Garth. A few seconds into the song, Malinda placed her left hand on his right shoulder. Then, Garth did the same to the person next to him. Malinda then stretched her right hand palm up toward the center of the circle. She took Garth's right hand and moved it out the same way. The people in the circle did the same. Malinda closed her eyes. She wanted to see what God was doing. She felt power flow through every person and saw many different colored lights flash throughout the entire room. She wanted to ensure that this circle was instructed by God. In thought, she asked, *what is this?* A Divine answer came, *this is your healing circle.* Malinda was able to relax and felt an intense presence of Christ. She prayed for all those standing with her that they be healed of all illnesses.

The music ended. Malinda opened her eyes. Cathy spoke and asked that the group pray for a seven year old boy who lived in B.C. who was dying of leukemia. Malinda prayed in spirit the words sent to her by DG. After the meeting, everyone went outside for a BBQ and lawn games.

After everyone left, Malinda retired to her bedroom. She changed into more comfortable clothes and thought about the healing circled when people meditated on God and she asked what that was. The answered quickened, "your healing circle."

Exhausted from the day's events, she went to bed and was later woken by a whisper, to open her bible. She knew it was the voice of God. She looked at the digital clock on her night table, then said, "it's 1:30 in the morning here. Let me sleep." But again the voice quickened the same message. Malinda got up knowing it would not leave her alone until she would open her bible. She walked to the living room and got her bible; sat down on a rocking chair. Randomly she opened the bible to a page titled Revelation of John chapter 2. John was her favorite gospel. Surprised that he wrote another book in the bible, she began to read a verse that referred to certain misbehaviors of a church in Pergamos. God describes his disapproval and warns to repent and change its ways. At the end of the message, it is written in verse 17, "He who has an ear, let him hear what the Spirit says to the churches. To him who overcomes I will give some of the hidden manna to eat. And I will give him a white stone, and on the stone a new name written which no one knows except him who receives it.'"

Malinda forgot all about her fatigue and tears flowed down her cheeks. She thought, *God actually gave me a real white stone. Then, everything he says in the bible is true. I will always cherish this present given by God.*

About three weeks later, Hubert phoned. He said, "Malinda, come over for coffee." Hubert had an excited tone to his voice, which Malinda was very familiar with. When she got to his place, he had a smile from ear to ear. "We had a visitor last night," he said.

"Oh yeah?" inquired Malinda.

"Yeah," he said. "A woman with a boy came to see the little house we have for rent. She explained that she was moving back from B.C. There was someone else with her. The woman explained that he was diagnosed with leukemia and had a rough time, but now he is completely recovered and the doctors can't explain how. They discharged him from cancer care. He'll still have to go for regular checkups just to be on the safe side."

"Wow!" exclaimed Malinda. "That's the boy we prayed for, isn't it?"

"Yes, I checked with Cathy and sure enough, it's him!"

Malinda was joyful. "I feel like dancing," she said. "I always feel like jumping up and dancing whenever something like that happens. This is God's doing. He doesn't always show us the result of our prayers but sometimes he does and this is one of those times. Isn't it great?" Hubert kept smiling, but now his smile was accompanied by a tear that ran down his cheek.

More people wanted to reside at Serenity House but could not because the location was not serviced by city transit. Six months after the grand opening, Roberta told Malinda that she saw the perfect Serenity House on TV. "What are you talking about?" asked Malinda.

"I was scrolling channels on TV this morning and stopped on the Real Estate channel and there it was! The perfect Serenity House. It's in the city and it's beautiful."

"Roberta, if it's that beautiful, then for sure I can't afford it," Malinda commented.

Later she looked at the property listing on the real estate website. That night, she went to bed unable to get the picture of the house out of her mind. The next morning, she called the real estate agent for a viewing. She brought Roberta and a couple of her other clients with her. Malinda told the agent she was going to think about it, and think about it she did. Roberta was right. It was perfect. She saw a newspaper ad about a bank that offered a lower interest rate for mortgages. She made an appointment and brought the real estate listing with her. Malinda was completely honest with the bank representative and figured that, since she had no income, the decision was going to be made for her. The rep would decline her request and that would be it for that risk. The opposite happened. The banker said, "I approve of what you are doing and there should be more places like these in this city. Your mortgage is approved. You have an excellent credit rating and as a rental investment, the property will produce enough income to make the monthly payments."

With her last three thousand dollars in savings, Malinda made a down payment on the house. There were three levels, each self-contained with kitchen, bedrooms, living room and three-piece bathroom. It was located in a safe area of the city. In no time, twelve residents were accepted to undergo a drug, alcohol and abuse recovery program. Some came from treatment facilities, rehab centers, hospital addiction units and psychiatric wards. Some escaped domestic abuses of all types and churches referred others. The majority was homeless. Malinda set up an office at the new Serenity House location and worked ten hours each day. Her brother, Hubert, sacrificed his time to do maintenance and repairs for a minimal fee. Malinda was on call twenty-four/seven. At times she had to attend emergencies and handle suicide attempts. The organization became a Canadian non-profit registered charity.

Malinda knew this was God-fated for at the end of the year 1999, her spousal support payments ended. As of January 1, 2000, her income went from $1,200 per month down to zero. In the autumn of that year, she owned and operated the transitional housing organization. She received no pay other than small honoraria. In the last year of operation, the government funded her modest salary. Much to her surprise, one day, DG affirmed she was to sell the property. *Housing Programs for addicts don't work any more. They will seek the Word of God.* Malinda had great difficulty to let go of the project and held onto it for one more year, during which time things became awful. Crystal Meth came into the picture. Most of the residents tried it or were hooked on it. The drug produced such rapid damage to their bodies that no program could have time to complete recovery before permanent damage to the brain was done or became fatal. Rehabilitation facilities did not have enough information about the substance to be able to develop effective recovery programs. The clients demonstrated psychoses and extreme episodes of violent aggression. Malinda burned out. Her financial picture worsened. For that year she accumulated several thousand dollars on a line of credit that she used to hang onto the facility. She was physically worn out and mentally stressed. She listed the property for sale and regretted not having done so a year sooner. On the bright side, the housing market rose 25% in the past three months. The property sold for more than the asking price. Malinda paid off the mortgage and her line of credit. She was once again debt free and still made a net profit of $35,000.

Malinda used the money sparingly and spent the next 3 months resting comfortably in her condo. During that time she marveled at God's mercy. Even though she did not immediately obey the directive to sell the property, God rescued her from all her financial burdens and gave her more than she could ever expect when she did as she was divinely directed. The most important lesson she learned as a result was that the next time DG instructed her to do something, she would avoid much turmoil by obeying right away.

Give It All Up

Aside from the long hours of work and other struggles, many good things happened at Serenity House. The most significant was about one of the residents named David who needed a liver transplant as a result of his misuse of alcohol and drugs. He also had Hepatitis C from using dirty needles to inject amphetamines. David was forty-two and had one son living in another province. His family and relatives would have nothing to do with him. Alcohol had taken his driver's permit, job, family and friends. Drug and alcohol abuse wanted to take his life. He came to Serenity House after being discharged from the hospital addiction unit and came straight from a twenty-eight-day stay at a provincial rehab centre. His doctor told him that he needed to be clean and sober for six months before beginning Hepatitis C treatments in order to be considered for a liver transplant. These were not all of his troubles. From birth, he was fatally allergic to bee stings and carried an Epipen with him at all times. Lastly, he had epilepsy. During his stay at Serenity House, he remained completely free of drugs and alcohol. Malinda only knew the sober David. He came to Serenity House one summer with nothing but the clothes on his back, which was a T-shirt, grey sweat pants and a pair of running shoes. Some days he felt well enough to help Hubert with painting and minor house repairs. He followed and respected the house rules and attended every program curriculum along with AA twice a week. During one of the house Twelve Steps faith meetings, a scripture was read in the Bible about a man having episodes of seizures similar to David's. Jesus healed him completely and his town people said that they had a hard time to recognize him because he remained calm, happy and cured of his violent seizures. On the evening of the reading, David decided to 'pass' when it was his turn to share, which was unusual for him. A few days later, a dinner and healing service were held at Serenity House with Malinda officiating. David stepped up and spoke saying, "If Jesus healed a man like the one we read about in the Bible, then he can cure me." Malinda placed her hand upon his head and the group prayed. At the next Twelve Steps meeting, David shared that he had no seizures that week and believed that he was completely cured of epilepsy. David stayed at Serenity House for a year and remained seizure free.

Another significant event for Malinda personally occurred during prayer at another meeting. She heard words in her spirit say, *Give it all up.* The group previously shared about their struggles with alcohol. Malinda knew what the statement meant. She had given up all alcohol consumption several years prior, except that she kept her most prized delight, which was a glass of wine with a meal. She reasoned that this was her reward after a demanding day at Serenity House. Her inner spirit knew that the call to *give it all up* was legitimate, but she would not forego such a small pleasure without a fight. For the next week, like a raging lioness that hangs on to its prey with locked jaws, Malinda confronted God by justifying the reasons why she should NOT give it up. An outburst of "buts" poured out like a ferocious river about to flood its banks as she attempted to convince herself. She criticized God, saying, *but I gave up all other alcohols. But I don't take drugs. But I only use the wine to enhance a meal. But it's my only reward after a day at the mission house. But I only have one glass and I do this only while eating a meal. But I gave up smoking, cussing and promiscuous sex. Surely I can keep this innocent drink. After all, it is known to produce medicinal effects that thin the blood for cardio vascular health. I drink it reasonably, only having 3 or 4 glasses a week.* After the rebellion, Malinda exhausted all the *buts* she could muster, after which she found herself with only that still small voice that offered no explanation. There was something about that inner voice that Malinda couldn't resist and she eventually caved in. Despite all the reasoning and logic she could muster, she knew she had to *give it all up.* When she did, she asked God to give one good reason why she had to give up the wine but no answer came.

After two weeks of abstaining from wine, one day after dinner, she was preparing a lesson to give at Serenity House. She was reading and found herself better able to continue the stronger positive thoughts of earlier in the day. She wondered what was different when she realized that she had had no wine. The answer to *why?* was revealed.

Part 3

Divine Intervention

Another noticeable effect of being free from all alcohol was that the absence of bouts of depression she experienced after having a glass of wine. The usual thoughts that surfaced in depression were about her father. With her mind clear, Malinda began to address her remaining resentments.

Nadine and Malinda went to church together one day. A miracle occurred that day when Malinda was completely healed from any and all bitterness toward her father. During the singing, Malinda closed her eyes and went to her inner place of peace with Christ. Suddenly she began to plead in her spirit, *I tried everything to soften my heart about my father.* She itemized every method used, naming therapy, written expressions of hatred, even going to her dad's gravesite and cussing words of anger, books and counseling suggestions. She began to weep and in prayer she said, *I even shouted at an empty chair.* She concluded that her Valentine's Day spiritual miracle of love expression to her dad was not real and told Christ, *even that was not enough.* She thought, I've done it all and even received a miracle. But now it's back. All resources to resolve this old issue had run out. Malinda was tired and fed up and gave up. As she continued her prayer, she said, *I am sorry I cannot forgive. I don't know how. You do. You do it. You forgive.*

Not a moment lapsed before she heard in her spirit, *truly I tell you there is not one burden I cannot carry for you.* At the same time a picture of Jesus on the cross appeared in her mind and quickened her spirit as she remembered the words that Jesus spoke while hanging from the cross with his body severely beaten beyond recognition. Swollen, bruised and bloodied, he declared to God, *"Father, forgive them for they know not what they do."* Malinda did not expect anything would result from sharing her plight with Jesus. She wanted to let Jesus know that she was done trying so hard to forgive, but the vision and words settled the matter once and for all. He asked God to forgive them. He gave it for God to do. She felt amazement at how Jesus actually took the residue of her unforgiveness and gave her His peace. She knew the scripture about asking and receiving, but never thought it was possible to ask Him to forgive for her. She thought it was her sole responsibility to bring herself to forgive and not something anybody else could do for her. All the years of her thinking that she must be a terrible person for not being able to wholeheartedly and completely forgive her dad had kept her in bondage with self-defeating thoughts. Her many attempts and failures to completely forgive made her believe that she was a rotten person, that it was futile to hope that some day she would be successful and forgive fully. When someone said good things about her father, she was free of the infuriating reaction of old anger.

Malinda never lost sight of her goal to heal and find what real love was. Her clean up of emotional debris had been like shoveling layers upon layers of dirt to find a great treasure. One by one, the outward reactive habits triggered by the past were hacked away at. The real foundational work was to tackle the inner habits of negative thinking, angers and fears. The healing of emotions assured that her destructive habits would stop and eventually find and open the treasure chest to get her deserved reward, which was love.

Mr. Hilton kept contact with Malinda and knew about some of her spiritual experiences. He phoned one day to ask if she would come to teach a course on channeling. Malinda responded, "What do you mean by channeling?"

"My Thursday evening class wants to know how to get supernatural direction for their personal life."

"Are you asking me to do psychic readings?" she asked.

Mr. Hilton answered, "You can design the course and name it what you want."

"I'll get back to you on that," concluded Malinda.

Later that day, Malinda asked DG during meditation if she should decline the invitation. That was what she really wanted to do but the answer was to accept. Malinda obeyed the direction and gave herself comfort by thinking that it would be an easy course to teach. She could copy the program that she regularly used and not have to prepare much for the course. *It would be good experience for me* she also thought; so she phoned Mr. Hilton back to accept the invitation and said, "I'll give a 3 week course and call it Divine Guidance. I'll do it for free."

The first class went quite smoothly. Mr. Hilton was there along with a dozen adult students. The room was the same one that Malinda attended when she herself was a student at the centre. Since her last visit at the centre, it had adopted a New Age course called getting what you want from God. During her first lesson, Mr. Hilton interrupted and declared, "God wants what you want." Malinda said, "God wants what you want when you want what God wants." The instructor was taken back and asked her to repeat her statement. After she did, he sat quietly and paid close attention to the remainder of her teaching. Malinda spoke about her inner healing process. At the end of the lesson, one student asked, "Show us how to connect with our soul." The others agreed. Their question was a valid one and they deserved a sound answer, but Malinda didn't have one. She told them that she would make the subject the next lesson's topic.

The next few days were spent trying to find a way to give the students a simple answer. Two days before the next class, Malinda had come up with nothing. She could not go back to the centre empty handed and she was getting nervous. She spent several hours reading her book notes and did not find any information on how to connect with one's soul. She could teach them simply to meditate until the peace of God is reached. Malinda knew that specific group had heard this kind of answer before and they would not be receptive to hearing about Christ. They had asked a hard question and Malinda was stuck for an answer. Time was running out. "How am I going to do that?" she reflected. The more she thought about devising a formula or a solution to the answer, the more she came up empty. At a total loss of ideas, there was only one thing left to do. She took her own advice which was to meditate and ask God but she doubted that an idea would turn up. It was her last hope. She went into prayer thinking that even if she received no direction that at least she would acquire the usual peace during the exercise and that alone would make the next two classes with this now difficult group, bearable. To relieve the pressure she felt, she focused on the fact that there were only two more classes and it would soon be over. *In the end*, she thought, *I am disappointing the students but I'll chalk it all up to experience.*

Before meditation she posed a precise question, "How do I show people how to connect with their soul?" As expected, there came no answer but Malinda was enjoying a state of complete peace. As soon as Malinda thought that her meditation was coming to a close, there appeared a simple but powerful reply to hold a light from upward while pointing it at the wall. Still in meditation, Malinda gleamed with joy and thought, *"How brilliant! Of course this would work! I'll point a flashlight at a wall. The light reflected on the wall would represent the soul and the flashlight would be God, the source."* Then DG corrected her to use a laser beam. "What's with the laser beam?" Malinda asked. DG. Immediately her answer came that a flashlight's light is too spread out and not direct enough. The more direct the beam, the less it is fragmented. Light from an ordinary light bulb cannot penetrate through a body like laser.

After the meditation, Malinda thought about how surgeons were using laser beams and about how x-rays can expose the inside of a physical body. Malinda came out of meditation feeling ecstatic. *This revelation is ingenious*, she thought and went to work immediately. She phoned her niece Cathy for her assistance to demonstrate the concept at the next class. Cathy helped design props for the demonstration. "I need you to draw a cut out figure of a person on paper about 5' in height," instructed Malinda. She explained the lesson to her niece. "I also need several pieces of paper cut into squares of 6 inch x 6 inch. On each, write these emotions, hurt, anger, fear, guilt, stress, anxiety."

There was only one thing left to complete the supplies. She needed a laser pointer. The last thing she wanted at this time was to spend money she didn't have. For the past couple of years she was living on the profit from the sale of the mission house. The device was new on the market and the price wasn't cheap. Thoughts flipped back and forth between Divine insight and her logic. It seemed strange that the all-knowing God would not consider the fact that she was not being paid for her time and costs but in the end, Malinda remembered the pain of deviating from God's master mind position.

She went to an office supply store. There were 4 different kinds of pointers on display and they were all marked down to 80% off. Although this might have been a pleasant surprise

Malinda thought that if this is God then she better not buy a junk. She approached a sales person and asked, "Are there more expensive pointers than those you have on display?" The sales person answered, "Nope; these are all we have. They are regularly priced at $80." For less than $20., Malinda took home the last piece of the material for her demonstration kit and was well prepared for the upcoming class.

Malinda was so excited about the demonstration that she invited her clients and friends but thought twice about calling Garth. She thought about how he only came to the city a few times a year because of distance but what Malinda was really hoping for was that he would not be available and decline her invitation. He might not be receptive to Malinda's teaching. She remembered her first preaching debut when Garth afterwards reprimanded her for not having used quotes from the bible and that he was used to teaching her instead. Malinda appeased her fear by reminding herself that Garth was not known to easily mingle with City folk and that he would probably not show up. In the end, she opted to trust that whoever was supposed to be there would show up so she invited him.

The next evening it was show time. Malinda and Cathy walked into the lobby of the counseling centre to find a room full of people. When they entered the teaching room, it was full also. On the right, were two full length couches and extra chairs were placed tightly against them. On the left wall were two rows of chairs and more were added in the middle of the room. All the chairs were used and it still wasn't enough. Some people sat on the floor in front of the whiteboard where Malinda stood. Some students had invited some of their friends to attend. Hubert and his wife were there also. Mr. Hilton sat at the doorway. Garth came in and sat at the back of the room.

After everyone settled down, Malinda introduced herself and Cathy. To break the ice, Malinda used an exercise which was received by DG a while back. She distributed a few hand held mirrors and asked that the participants take turns for there weren't enough to go around. She instructed them to hold the mirror gently against their nose. In the mirror, some saw their two eyes as one. Some giggled at what the mirror reflected they looked like. One fellow named Steeve was a student when Malinda attended the centre as a student herself. He was the one that had played the role of counselor back when Malinda broke down in tears when she talked about her daughter's accident. He didn't normally feel emotion. He was a victim of severe childhood abuse and learned to disassociate from his feelings. He was going through a divorce and moved out of his home. He was unemployed, depressed, alienated from his children and didn't have a friend in the world. He continued to attend sessions at the center in the hopes to reconnect with his feelings.

Steeve had a noticeable reaction to the mirror exercise. He laughed uncontrollably. Curious about what he was experiencing Malinda asked him what he found so funny. As though he could not hear her, Steeve kept laughing and ignored the person next to him who was waiting for her turn to have the mirror. Malinda called out his name and asked again, "why are you laughing?" Steeve tried to answer but couldn't describe what he was experiencing. Malinda was surprised that someone thought the exercise was that funny. Finally Steeve said something. "I don't know," he replied. Then, Mr. Hilton shouted from the back of the room, "He's feeling an emotion," "What do you mean, he's feeling an emotion," Malinda asked. "His laughter," Mr. Hilton responded, "He is releasing an emotion – humor!" The exercise helped to revive someone whom, for years, was emotionally dead.

For others the exercise helped them to realize that what they see in the mirror about themselves is not always how they really are. They shared about how the mirror reflected two images – one up close and a different one when holding the mirror at a distance. The analogy was used to indicate how a person can view themselves as both confident and self assured or sub-standard and lowly when looking at their mirror image and how, for example, anorexia can project a skinny person's imagery to be fat or even obese. One person said, "I'll never depend on a mirror to tell me what I am. From now on, I'm going to look to my inner child for that answer which is something that my mirror can't perceive."

The group was intrigued and their interest about how to connect with their soul rose with anticipation. Cathy brought her paper cut out to the front and pinned him up on the wall. She turned to the group and said, "This is Mike." The class answered back, "Hi Mike." Malinda spent a few minutes recapping the previous class for those who were absent the week before. She finished by saying that this demonstration will provide an example that the inner child needs a clean up process and how to connect with the soul. Cathy then got the little square papers with negative emotions written on them. She held the pack at Mike's center of his body while Malinda explained that the papers indicated the emotional condition that Mike worked on during his healing process. She took out the laser pointer from her pocked and stepped back a few feet. She shown the device on the top paper with the word Hurt written on it and explained that Mike worked on his hurts and peeled off the many layers of negative emotions he had. Cathy removed the top card to reveal the next which revealed the word Anger. Malinda shown the pointer on it and explained that after the light pointed on Mike and he became aware of his anger issues and worked on those until his many fears surfaced. Cathy removed the top card and revealed the next with the word Guilt written on it. The next few cards had the words worry, stress and anxiety on them. Malinda explained how fear, anger and guilt led to stress and how these conditions may be causing physical illnesses.

Malinda explained how God is Spirit and knows where healing is needed and shines His light on the area. The light produces healing," Malinda declared. After that area is healed, if the subject wants to continue the healing journey, the Holy Spirit touches the next obstruction of a person with light. The little red dot from the laser pointer shown on the paper cards demonstrated how the light helped to heal Mike's past hurts. When that was done Mike was decontaminated from his past emotional toxicity. Having no more old baggage to carry around he was freed. Malinda said, "The term lighten-up fits well in this descriptive example of someone unloading a weighted past. No longer trapped in the past, Mike was freed from emotional captivity"

Malinda asked, "What is the beam of light working on?" Someone yelled, "Mike." With the papers out of the way, the light now pointed directly on Mike. "Are you getting the gist of this demonstration?" asked Malinda. She explained, "There were no more obstructions (the emotion papers) that could keep Mike from being connected to the source of light. The unhealed wounds kept the light from shining directly onto his soul. The channel is now clear. The reception can be heard clearly because it is coming from within!" She smiled and looked at her students. One woman in the room particularly had a remarkable change in her eyes. Malinda said to her, "your eyes are shining with light; you are gleaming. What happened?" The woman answered, "You are speaking to my very soul." Malinda admitted to the group, "During my life, the pure light was revealed to me only sporadically and usually during times of deep burden. I didn't know what it really was at the time." Malinda told the class about the night she was rescued from her husband threatening to kill her and she saw the white light afar in a dark tunnel. "When I entered my healing process, I could see that light guiding me to reveal God to me." Malinda's eyes were now gleaming but it was not enlightenment the cause but tears. She closed the demonstration and said, "I am so thankful for the light of God."

Garth had a temper. He cleared his throat and paused as he prepared to speak. Malinda waited as she gripped the laser pointer tighter in her sweaty hand. Malinda thought that because the name Jesus was not mentioned, Garth had nothing to loose in criticizing her demonstration. Malinda thought the worst. She prepared herself for the coming public embarrassment by challenging her with a question relating to the bible.

Garth's strong voice resonated from the back of the room. "The laser is the source of the light. From the source all the way to Mike there was no visible beam. Because a beam could not be seen it doesn't mean it's not there." Then, Mr. Hilton said, "We tend to believe only what the physical eye sees." Malinda added, "Right; because it is not something that can be seen, communication with Divine can be disbelieved. The laser is the source of light which is symbolic to God. A quartz battery provides the energy which is symbolic to God's spirit. Batteries produce energy. God's power is energy." Malinda asked if anyone had any questions. A student answered, "Nope. It's pretty clear to me." Mr. Hilton thanked Malinda and Cathy. The classroom emptied. Garth waited for Malinda in his car. When Malinda walked out, he rolled down his window and said, "People need demonstrations like that to understand. I have to hurry and head back up north. Good-bye."

Heal Thyself Back to Love

The next day, Hubert called to invite Malinda over for supper. He said, "Now I have something to tell you that is very interesting."

"Of course, I'll go," said Malinda with an enthusiastic tone. At 4:30, Malinda rushed over to Hubert's house. His wife had prepared a special dinner. As they all ate, Hubert announced that afterwards they would sit in the living room where it would be more comfortable to talk. After dinner, Malinda was the first to sit on the couch. She exclaimed, "come on, Hubert, I can't wait any more." Hubert sat on his recliner. He said, "Our cousin Roger showed me a genealogy on the family. Grandmother on dad's side was a Métis. Her mother, our great grandmother, was a pure blooded Cree Indian. When she died, her husband would not or could not care for the children. Grandmother was raised in an orphanage run by nuns. At the time, it was shameful to be native. Malinda exclaimed, "Grandpa married a half breed?"

"Yep." answered Hubert.

"But Grandpa hated Indians," Malinda continued.

"Yep," commented Hubert

"You mean, he died never knowing that he married one?" stated Malinda while clapping her hands. Hubert had an expression of pleasing calculation on his face and added, "Yep!"

Later, Malinda did some of her own research. She found that her Métis roots dated back to the birth of the country's nation. The Indians were the first inhabitants of Canada. French Europeans moved in and married Indian women. Those people were known as the Métis nation. When the Dominion Government of Canada was formed, it dismissed aboriginal culture and its history as worthless and inferior. The Indians and Métis called on an educated Métis man named Louis Riel and formed an army with the Indians. They declared themselves the provisional government of Assiniboia and took over Fort Garry. Louis Riel then continued to negotiate

Manitoba's entry into Confederation. Riel was after language guarantees, and the land rights. The Canadian government sent a force of 1200 British troops and volunteers. They banished Riel for five years, but Riel kept slipping in and out of French communities in southern Manitoba. Eventually he was hung in Regina in 1885 for staging a second rebellion in the territory that would later become Saskatchewan. Soon after, residential schools were built. Indians and Métis children were taken out of their homes to place them in society for the purpose of racial indoctrination. Later Louis Riel was named "Father of Manitoba." The residential schools shut down and some of them were torn down by the band councils on the reserves.

This history lesson was significant to Malinda. She was aware that a number of families in Ste. Agnes were half breeds and Métis. The customs and traditions she grew up with derived from the Métis. Old time jigging music and fiddling were favorite activities. A language of slanged French was spoken which Malinda now understood was in fact "Métif." Hunting, trapping and berry picking were aboriginal practices passed down by the first nation's people. Agnes and the many towns surrounding the area swarmed with Métis people who hid their social class or didn't know their family history. The revelation of Malinda's family history fit perfectly within the scope of her healing journey by completing the missing pieces of her identity and understanding her childhood customs.

Love had been the reason for beginning her journey and step-by-step Malinda walked her way back to love. She resolved to accept her entire make-up just as she was in every part of her being which included her biological background, personality, temperament, qualities, weaknesses, disposition, spirit and every hair of her moral fiber. To love herself back to health was as important as breathing. "Heal thyself back to Love," was a statement divinely revealed to her. Those 4 words spoke a million affirmations as she peeled the onion layer by layer on her way back to love as though travelling through hills, mountains, rivers, rocky roads and even a pit like following a treasure map leading to a valuable buried chest. Malinda achieved complete acceptance of all she knew about herself.

A few weeks later, on December 16th Malinda enjoyed the pleasant surroundings of the Christmas atmosphere in her condo.

She sat comfortably in her wing chair beside the living room window where she could see the star lit sky. As she looked at her condo's Christmas decor, she filled her thoughts with the Christmas décor in her childhood home. She remembered a particular advent calendar of long ago when she opened the perforated edges of the same date – December 16th long past. Malinda was just a few weeks shy of her 6th birthday. The memory brought her to when she was asleep that night when suddenly, she awoke and saw a pair of skinny legs standing beside her bed. Malinda was groggy but recognized that it was her father. She didn't know what he was doing there but then, he put one hand over her mouth and with his other hand he fondled her vagina. He lay on top of her and penetrated her with his engorged penis. Even though this caused Malinda great physical pain, she dared not utter a sound.

She remembered how her eyes felt like they were going to erupt out of their sockets. Blood raced through her body and rushed to her head. Her skull felt like it was going to explode. Her ears were ringing and felt like they were about to bleed. Sweat came out of every pore on her body. Her skin felt red hot. Her hips tensed up tightly so that the bones could resist the intrusion and keep from breaking. She felt something inside her vagina tear and she passed out. When she woke again, her father was rubbing her forehead with a wet, cold face cloth. She heard him say, "Stay quiet." Malinda inhaled and smelled an odor of whiskey. When her father left the room Malinda turned on her side to check on her 3 year old sister in a matching twin bed. She was sound asleep. Malinda cried quietly.

In the morning Malinda was in pain and stayed in bed. Her hips ached and her vagina was inflamed. She heard the older children leave for school. Her mother did not tend to her wounds. Later, she heard her dad come in the house. She got up to look for him. She found him in the living room just about to turn on the television. Malinda walked up to him and faced him gallantly and stood directly facing him. She looked up and bluntly said, "Why did you do that to me?" She truly believed that he would answer a sincere explanation but instead he retorted, "*vas-ten d'icit*" which means, "Get out of here!" Her father towered over her and his bad-tempered reaction scared her away. She was stunned and puzzled. As she walked away her entire body was still hurting.

She returned to her bed and thought that her father would later explain everything and he would never do that again. Everything would be normal again. It was a weekday and Malinda stayed home from school for the remainder of the week. Her dad did not talk to her nor acknowledged her presence.

That week, Malinda went to her mother for help and told her that her "pipi" was really sore. Her mother's reaction was even more difficult to understand. She said nothing and did nothing. Now Malinda was being ignored by both parents. Malinda thought about how earlier that year, her mother nursed her back to health from the measles. She tended to her attentively then but Malinda could not understand why this ailment was not important. Malinda decided to approach her again. The next day while the older siblings were in school, she went to her mother where she was sitting in her rocking chair darning socks. Malinda complained about her pain but her mother kept at her knitting as though Malinda wasn't there. Malinda was determined to get attention for her ailments. Malinda told her mother that she needed help. The silence broke and her mother said, "Don't bother me with your problems."

Her attempts to get help had only annoyed her mother and upset her father. She didn't tell any of her siblings what their daddy had done to her. Still, Malinda was afraid that she ripped inside and the aching hipbones would not heal. That fear compelled her to try one final time. She returned to her mother to get her to mind the wounds. This time she used a different approach. In a defiant way she posed a new question and asked her mother, "Why don't you do something?" Her mother could no longer ignore the girl's relentlessness and answered the question with a nonchalant tone, *Celui qui a l'argent a le pouvoir,*" which means, "He who has the money has the power." Malinda walked away. It was evident her mother put a "period" to that statement and would not pursue the topic. Malinda left even more bewildered than before.

Malinda was robbed of the happiness that surrounded her Christmas joy. That Christmas she kept to herself and cried much of the time. Eventually the physical pain from the incident went away. Her brothers and sisters seemed to not have noticed anything about what had happened. Every ritual detail of Christmas went on schedule as customarily planned and in its usual manner.

In her condo that night, the new Malinda was smoke and alcohol free, practiced healthy eating and exercised regularly. Malinda was fit spiritually, physically and mentally. An event too horrible for a young child to handle had been pushed way to the deepest part within and covered the first layer of dirt on top of her valued treasure chest. The dirt free Malinda was now able to remember and her wonderful Christmas memories were changed forever.

The rape hurt Malinda physically and her father's rejection wounded her emotionally. Her mother's reaction changed her understanding into believing that *she* was a badly behaved child. Unable to make a clear judgment of the experience, Malinda locked the wounded child within. The inner Malinda was not only covered with a layer of dirt but also imprisoned. Her mind was tricked but everywhere Malinda went, she was accompanied by that little inmate locked in a jail cell within. That rape was locked away but the emotional effects remained free from internal incarceration. Thinking back, being successful at getting people's approval and pleasing others was evidence that she was loved. She subconsciously avoided silence to keep from hearing the cries of the inner Malinda. When alone, she'd make sure that a radio, stereo or TV was on. When anger surfaced it was numbed with alcohol. She would not trust anyone and so the cigarette became her best friend. She fought relentlessly to keep her first husband even though he was badly behaved. When she quit smoking, food replaced the lost friendship.

Malinda turned to her older sister Georgette for guidance but Georgette regarded her father to be a perfect example of a loving parent. Malinda struggled with the idea and hoped that Georgette could convince her otherwise. Malinda viewed her mother as discontented with her husband and Georgette made allegations that her mother was ungrateful. Malinda saw her mother recluse to her bedroom for hours and several days would go by without hearing her talk to her husband. In such times, Georgette took charge of her mother's duties. Malinda tried to make sense of her opposing viewpoint. She noticed that her father ignored his wife just as he did Malinda. Mother's birthday passed without recognition so

Georgette would get permission from her dad to buy a gift on his behalf. Georgette often tried to maintain harmony between her parents and refused to believe the obvious dysfunction in the couple's relationship. Malinda watched the interactions of her family carefully and knew that the children had no power to make the parents get along. When Mother resumed the function of caring for her husband Georgette forfeited her role as household manager and handed it back to her mother.

Malinda wanted to believe more what Georgette said than what she knew. She wanted to believe that everything was okay, so she listened and ignored her own eyes. When she was a teen, Malinda asked Georgette, "why is being kind to a wife and children not required from a father?" Georgette answered, "You're 15 years old and you sorely think that dad doesn't love you." Malinda stood her ground with the comment, "then why can't he say that he loves us? Lorraine's dad said it to his family. I heard him say it"

Georgette argued, "of course dad loves us. Can't you see how hard he works?" The doubting Malinda stood her ground and said, "Lorraine's dad works hard too!"

Georgette straightforwardly said, "You were a child that needed too much attention." With that said Georgette was able to convince Malinda that she was a demanding child and decided to also lock doubt away. But Malinda vowed that she wanted a different love than that of her parents'. She would marry someone that paid attention to her feelings and needs. He would care about his family in addition to providing for them with money. He would not be cold but be able to say, I love you. Her prince in shining armor would be gallant.

With the recollection of the rape, Malinda was able to view her father truthfully and knew more than before the importance of correcting the lies of her past. She came to terms with the memory and its effects on her life. Memories about even the smallest thing began to take on significance. For instance, during her teen years Malinda had a favorite song she loved to sing called, "Silence is Golden." She had been attracted to that song without much thought about why. Now she realized she had taken the message in the song and adopted it as her proven method to not cause problems. During the trauma, she had been told to be silent. That old dogma got knocked down and gave birth to a new belief that when sexually abused, silence is NOT golden. Also her view about sex was directly linked to being sexually violated. The lack of sexual restraint that Malinda's father demonstrated taught her that sex was an act as a result of an uncontrollable feeling rather than an act of trust and consent.

Malinda still struggled with self-loathing in response to other people's bad acts. She realized that she had always taken the blame for things, even when others made bad choices that affected her. Her inner chatter was still a problem, especially when someone said or did something even mildly abusive toward her, the reaction of self-loathing would re-surface. But now with the memories of incest clearly visible in her mind, Malinda gave name to the intermittent and unexplainable outbursts during her adulthood to be, "incest bouts." The recall gave a new discovery of how although remembering was painful, it was as though her emotional pain could remember the rape while her conscious brain did not. Throughout her life, she adopted her father's demeaning verbal statements as her own. His echoes resounded within her negative self worth. During incest bouts his loathing words repeated "get out!" and the inexplicable neglect from her mother along with her messages to, "leave me alone," and, "don't bother me with your problems," were so haunting.

Malinda was well into her late forties, when on the anniversary of the incest, December 16th. she saw the memory in her mind and felt like it had just happened. During the flashback she was consumed with rage and felt an enormous amount of fury toward her deceased father. She blamed him for causing even greater damage than his destructive criticisms and displays of his physical violence. She could not contain those feelings. The remembrance came as a complete surprise. She was unprepared for this and her own anger scared her. It reminded her of the time when she spoke to her two last cigarettes in her car and threw them out the window. Then, she had something physical to throw but this time she didn't have that for this problem. She knew to call for help and made an appointment to see Dr. Fiji. She told the doctor about remembering the incest. The doctor listened to Malinda let out all of the memories and connections she was making. When she was finished, Malinda said "I want you to refer me to a specialist that deals with incest," she asked.

"This psychiatrist comes highly recommended and works with abuse victims," the doctor said as she wrote down a name and number to call.

"Thanks," said Malinda; "I want to talk to someone who understands," she added. As a result of her recent education on abuse, the therapy she received and making time each day for meditative prayer, a breakthrough took place. Now Malinda was able to convert the belief that in that situation, yelling was VITAL and was not a bad thing to do. She adopted a new belief that "yelling can save my life."

Being clear-headed, in the days to follow, other memories became lucid. Another was a time when Malinda was 8. She was angry and headed down the main road just past her driveway. She was determined about running away when Hubert rode up to her on his bike. He asked, "Where yah going?"

"I don't care!" Malinda answered.

"What if a bad guy picks you up?" Hubert asked.

Again, Malinda answered, "I don't care!" but added, "At least I won't be here!" Hubert thought to scare her into returning back home. "Big wolves from the woods are going to come out and eat you," he said with a tone of horror. Malinda looked at the woods on each side of the road. Hubert continued, "You know, when they want to kill there's a bunch of them that circle you and then the biggest wolf attacks."

Malinda stopped walking and said, "You're making that up just to scare me, aren't you?"

"No, really, it's true. I read it in my hunting magazine." Hubert confirmed.

"Now the biggest wolf that kills you is the first one that gets to eat before all the others. He has the biggest fangs and rips your skin to get to the meat. When he's finished eating, the rest finish you up until there's nothing left." Hubert concluded. Malinda paused then said, "You know what dad does to me." Hubert answered, "But out here, worse things will happen to you." Malinda hesitated for a moment then turned around and walked back. From that moment, Malinda accepted her lot in life and went back home.

This memory showed Malinda why she stayed in bad situations and kept repeating the same bad choices like going to her sister for advice only to get an opinion of how she kept messing up. Also why she did not leave Brian at the first sign of violence during their dating and later believed his statement that no one else would want a woman with two children. Knowing the cause of her adult behaviors was bittersweet. On one hand, she was finally able to identify the root of a problem which eased the process of eradicating the harmful behavior but on the other hand, she felt the hurt and cried about being powerless when she turned back from running away from an injurious situation and accepted to put up with her father.

Malinda began to clean up emotionally on a new level. She decided to go through another "housecleaning" and removed some people from her circle of friends that, although they were sober, used verbal abuse when they didn't get their way. Working on her own negative chatter was a daily procedure as she strived to make her new beliefs habitual and her inner strength increased. One friend in particular was Roberta. She became popular with Malinda's other friends but also she became moody and clingy. She could not spend a day without several phone calls to Malinda and a chance to be with her. When Malinda spent time with someone else, Roberta became jealous. One evening they were at a movie theatre when Roberta snuggled her head on Malinda's shoulder and stroked her knee. Malinda was very uncomfortable and told her she was not like that. Malinda gave herself permission to run away. Malinda cut the relationship. Roberta was outraged and tried to turn several others against her. Malinda lost a few of her other friends along the way. That was a difficult period to go through but Malinda valued her freedom more than to become a prisoner of that circumstance in order to gain approval. In the end, Malinda became more powerful in warding off her own self-loathing thoughts and was able to judge new situations better.

When she thought about the poor choices of her past Malinda turned her thinking around. Being thankful that the memory losses had come to light was painful but rewarding. She was able to forgive her own past behavior of being pathetically needy of approval. Most important that she no longer kept troublesome issues bottled up inside.

The incest bouts became less frequent. Malinda put into a right perspective a simple but formerly fearful lesson that there is a time and a place for yelling, screaming, crying and saying no; at times even to run away. For the first time as long ago as her preschool years, the emotional stability she so desperately wanted was back. Her outcries that she learned to be bad behavior in childhood turned out to be the necessary tools she needed to prevent abuse. The reconstruction of her behavior now included the wisdom to know when to use an objection.

She felt an enormous progress but she deeply needed to hear her father say he was sorry. That was not possible. She yearned for his hug that would follow his remorse. She wanted a kind daddy and to be told with heartfelt meaning that he would never do that again. She thought it only fair to expect closure by the one who had done the damage. This would never be possible, she thought, *he's dead*. Malinda read about letting go of false expectations and that if she didn't, her dad would continue to have power over her even though he was gone. She adopted a new mantra that things are not always fair. She rose to a higher level of thinking that her emotional success was not the result of everything going perfectly but was her will to move forward no matter what had happened in the past. With Divine Guidance, Malinda was able to get honest with herself and take full responsibility for her own adult choices.

During the last portion of Malinda's healing journey some relapses occurred and an incest bout would upset her. At times, lengthy episodes of crying were exasperating. Sometimes she cried for days. She felt a different old emotional pain in the pit of her stomach. It was the location in her anatomy that Malinda identified as the center of her soul. It was an area that had no visible matter but had a substance of spirit. It was home to where the need to be loved resided. At the same time, it was the place where the old memory of incest was uncovered. Malinda let out as many tears as needed to flow. These were old tears that should have been cried decades ago. Hurt that was caused by her daddy's incest act floated away within the tears.

Malinda was easily triggered even when watching television while viewing a father's gentle hand toward a daughter. The continuum started with a gut retching pain; then, thoughts flooded her mind that no one even hugged her during her childhood. Old destructive thoughts followed all the while crying her eyes out. This time she would not suffocate her feelings or the pain but let the flow of pain pass through her system. She had full awareness that using harm to eliminate harm was senseless and knew what it would take to stay away from her former ways of getting comforted. With each trigger she let the pain process and the incest bouts lessened.

Malinda walked through her dark valley. She was completely out of denial. At times the emotional pain was so severe that it made her physically sick. Her eyes were read and swollen from crying. The next morning, she woke up with a throbbing sinus headache and woke up more tired than before she had gone to bed. The aftermath of an incest bout reminded her of a hangover after a drunk. It was fitting to name this adverse effect an "emotional hangover." During the bouts, nothing she had learned to do to relieve this type of pain seemed to work. When she was tempted to think of herself as a failure she had something else going for her. She had the vision when Jesus held her hand to help her stand. She prayed for help and that never failed to ease the pain. She remembered in the vision that he was the love she had always searched for. He was the knight in shining armor.

With a boisterous voice, Malinda affirmed that she would never again abuse herself with negative thoughts. After she applied for a job and got rejected, old thoughts returned and beat herself up about how nobody wanted her and that she was going to end up on welfare. Once, she prayed and said to God, "Christians are supposed to have peace inside them. Divine Guidance was quiet and no answer came.

She found the answer while reading her Bible. The same day she asked, "Why do I still have negative thoughts and don't have peace?" a section of scripture from the New Testament was read from Gospel of John, chapter 14; verse 27, where Jesus said, *Peace I leave with you; my peace I give you. I do not give to you as the world gives. Do not let your hearts be troubled and do not be afraid.*

That evening Malinda continued her heart felt talk with God. She was angry and said, "How is it that I am afraid of not being wanted. How is it that I am a Christian, willing to get better and wants to follow your teachings but still I have a deep hurt inside me that just won't go away? I asked you to remove this pain but you don't?" She was being honest to the core about her confession of hurt and the injustice which she was going through. She got angry and again thought about how men had hurt her. She waited for an answer from

God but again there was that empty silence. She went to bed that night with old feelings of loneliness that sparked reminders that she lived alone and cannot find anybody to love her.

The next day, she attended a funeral at an aboriginal Anglican church. Initially she didn't want to go but couldn't refuse the invite when her friends from the reserve told her that it was important to them that she goes. On her way there, Malinda continued to feel lonely and wished she had a husband to attend the event with her. She said to Jesus, "I'm tired of having to go to places by myself." A correcting thought quickened in her spirit that she had no other place to go anyway. Then the right way of thinking kicked in and she was okay about going, even by herself.

At the funeral there were about 70 Aboriginals from their community. Malinda was the only non- treaty in attendance. Malinda knew only her friend, Lloyd, an aboriginal pastor, his wife and a couple of his friends. She entered the church and spotted a seat but much to her dismay it was beside a grumpy old man who hated all whites, Métis included. He was the last person she wanted to sit beside but it was the only chair in the house available. Malinda approached him and said, "Hello." The old man grumbled a moaning sound. "The church is full," Malinda said as she tried to be polite. The old man turned his head away. Malinda thought, *this may be an opportunity to practice forgiving and loving your enemy*. She soon accepted him just as he was and left him alone for the duration of the funeral.

After the burial, a buffet style dinner of the women's home cooking was served in the hall. Malinda sat with her pastor friend. It was unusually quiet during dinner. If someone spoke, it was in a low tone and at times some laughter could be heard.

Malinda's first nation friends were gentle and mild-mannered. The older children showed respect for their elders by serving a plate of food to them first. After the older people were all served, the rest of the people got up to get their meal. It was heartwarming to witness teenagers having high regard for their aged population. During the quiet of the gathering, Malinda found that it was a place of respect and love, answering her prayer. There, she was shown God's peace.

Scattered bits of repressed memories came back to Malinda. Now that she was facing the painful reality at times she wondered if her recalls were real. Bits and pieces of certain events resurfaced and more pieces of the puzzle came together. The recollections kept gnawing at her to experience and process. One time, she even wondered if the terrible recall could have come from a past life. At least then, she would have an explanation and would not have to deal with the memories. But being completely out of denial she couldn't ignore the anguish of the locked memories and set them free to remembrance. During those years of darkness, Malinda lived not only hurtfully but there were some good memories of her childhood that also needed to be freed. Both types of memories found their way back and reattach to their fragmented parts.

Now that she was facing the painful reality, she decided to share her story to help encourage and support others with similar experiences. She was asked to speak to a group about incest. Parts of her unexposed past were now out in the open. You could hear a pin drop when she told about her most enlightening and perplexing issue of knowing why her father would push her away and could not make eye contact with her. "It was a bittersweet finding," she said, "to know that the reason was because when he looked at me, he saw his guilt," she concluded. A question from the floor was asked. "When did you know that you had no memory for a certain period of your life?" Malinda told about when she was just under 10, the phone rang and Georgette answered the call. There wasn't much talking going on. After the call Georgette announced that mother had a baby boy. There was excitement in the house. "But my reaction was different. I was shaken by the news. I never noticed that my mother was pregnant," she told. "That moment remained with me ever since with a haunting question that had no answer. How is it possible that a girl, nearly ten years old would not know that her mother was pregnant?"

Malinda continued and said, "The only thing I remembered was the ringing sound of the telephone that day and I heard that mom had a baby was the moment I "returned" and again began to notice my surroundings. I always knew there was something wrong with my memory that I could not remember nearly five years of my life. I never told anybody because I was afraid to be known as someone who had something wrong mentally. When Lorraine and I would get together and she would reminisce about some mischievous adventure we had together as children, I pretended I remembered. But I wondered why I had absolutely no recollection. I was mentally messed up."

After the talk, Malinda was sipping on a cup of coffee when a woman well into her seventies stood close beside her and whispered, "My father used to rape me too. I never told anybody up until now. It feels good to finally let it out." As the woman told a bit of her story, Malinda thought that for her to experience such a confession and to see the 50 or 60 years of anguish from a deep and dark secret leave this woman confirmed Malinda that telling her story will help others.

The rape explained medical problems as well as emotional problems in her life. The hysterectomy Malinda had at a young age and for years afterwards, the result of the operation baffled Malinda. The surgeon described that her uterus which was removed had multiple damage. One of them was that unexplained scar tissue. The cervix is not open except during childbirth, so Malinda believed that perhaps the rape caused the tear which would explain the ripping pain Malinda felt inside her during the rape, just before she passed out.

About 20 years after the hysterectomy, during a physical exam, unusual cells had been discovered where her cervix used to connect to the uterus. Tests concluded the cells were malignant. Malinda wondered if the cells were also a result of the physical damage done inside the vaginal wall. It was determined that a biopsy would be performed to determine what kind of cancer treatment Malinda would need to undergo. At the time, Malinda's faith had grown stronger and she believed God could and would heal this cancer. During a biopsy the doctor was puzzled that he no longer could find the abnormal cells. They had disappeared. Malinda believed that God performed his own operation and protected Malinda from cancer.

Malinda's hostility toward her deceased father ran the gamut from why her childhood was so difficult to understand, to the physical damages of her body. She shouted, "How dare he judge Brian and point out his inadequacies, when he was no better. At least my husband was not a hypocrite and always admitted to his wrongdoings. Who proved to be the better man? I hate hypocrisy more than being beaten by my husband!"

The last piece of the unsolved puzzle started to come together. One in particular was that she often wondered why she felt no pain or had no bleeding from loosing her virginity to Brian compared to the stories other girls told about their loss. Malinda secretly kept to herself but justified her uneventful first time to slipping off her boy's bicycle pedal when she was younger and banged her crotch on the straight bar. This was something she heard in junior school that a girl said could happen. The majority of girls experience bleeding and pain but bleeding may not necessarily occur, one magazine article described. Neither explanation satisfied Malinda's inquisition. There was always a recurring whisper that hinted she lost her virginity differently.

Tears Remember

During an appointment with her psychiatrist, Malinda exclaimed, "My dad made a fool out of me!" She raised her voice with fury and said, "How dare he criticize my husband and encourage my family to hate Brian by playing the "poor me," role. Had I remembered what he did to me, I would NOT have blamed my husband for provoking a fight on my wedding night. I probably would have condoled, even sent him and his gang to give him the beating he so deserved." It was just her anger talking. After she calmed down, she began to cry and said, "Of course I would not have wanted my daddy hurt in any way, no matter what he did.". The doctor responded, "You are expressing certain feelings for the first time and it is going to sound like it is going to sound." Malinda then allowed herself to remember and release any emotions that were locked up and disallowed to run their natural course. "I've been angry most of my life. When he hurt me I wanted to scream. I wanted to tell him off and my mom too for not hearing me," Malinda said as she pulled a tissue out of her purse and wiped her tears. The emotions attached to her past traumatic events were finally given a voice. When she returned home Malinda drifted quietly to sleep on her couch, spent from crying and venting.

The year after working through the recovered memories of that event, Malinda moved to a beautiful country home adjacent to a boreal forest. Two days after the move, she was tired from unpacking and took a break. She headed outside to explore her new paradise. It was fall. The day was warm yet very windy. There was a creek that ran through the back of the property. As she walked along side the waters, she came to a stop and stood on its highest point overlooking a vast area of meadow land. She spread out her arms and enjoyed the sound of the wind as it blew through her short hair. The gusts of strong breeze reminded her of a relaxation method she once used of the desert wind and the sand blowing about only now she heard and felt the real wind. She closed her eyes and pretended the wind was blowing away all her scrambled thoughts when, all of a sudden, she felt an overpowering urge to scream. The closest neighbor was half a mile away and the wind blew the opposite direction. Malinda felt safe to let it all out. She screamed. After which she took a deep breath and lamented out another yell. The emotional pain of incest was loud and lengthy. Tears began to flow that seemed to come from the depths of her heart and out to her tear ducts. More pent up pain and memories from decades of emotional distress were released. She felt a simultaneous effect of healing both in the physical as well as emotional. The liberation freed the memories to remember as the cries for help which were long in captivity were at last allowed. It was as though her tears remembered also. Standing on the edge of the creek, Malinda used the adult to cry woes from the child within the wound as the lost five years of childhood memories took place.

Knowing this piece of the puzzle, her previously missing memories, explained many things that Malinda had wondered about during her life. Malinda processed the interaction with her father, and his fears, after her own. She understood that her father belittled her because he was guilty and afraid she would tell.

When he disapproved of her husband to others it kept Malinda from being believed should she disclose to Brian her father's dark secret. Maybe pride or fear of how the community viewed him kept him from making amends to Malinda. She realized that he too made a prison cell for himself to hide the truth. He was a prisoner of his daughter's same incest but his inner incarceration was for committing the crime. Her father's unwillingness to reveal the truth prevented not only her healing from happening but also his own.

Malinda had a perplexing truth that she was now facing. Previously she could not tell the truth simply because she did not remember it but her father did not know that fact. Malinda felt sorry for her dad when she thought about how he must have lived in constant fear and worried about who she could have told. Should that ever happen, in order to prevent the truth from being believed, his hiding made him go further by convincing others that Malinda was just a troublemaker that married another troublemaker. The fear of his daughter disclosing the truth must have haunted him terribly, Malinda thought. She told her psychiatrist, "He must have been tormented something fierce. To keep others from believing me, he said mean and false things about me. He repeatedly said I was no good for nothing and a constant troublemaker."

"How did that affect you?" asked the doctor. "It obviously affected my schoolwork. The nuns reported to my mom that I was excessively inattentive and that I purposely ignored work assignments. In my third grade, I went from straight A's and B's to straight F's. I failed my grade 3. From that I learned that I was stupid and a failure. By the time puberty hit, I lived up to my father's accusations and became a troublemaker at school. Then, I also failed grade 9. I realize now that I actually helped him to reinforce and further proved that I was trouble. I think about the fact that if I would have remembered the incest, it would still be to no avail. He simply could have reminded everyone what a problem I was."

"I came to believe those lies about myself. The battle raged for a long time. My father's belittling and blaming led me to make up my own reasons why I felt that my daddy did not love me." Malinda continued. "As a small child, I interpreted that it was because I was ugly, too skinny and restless," she concluded. The psychiatrist asked, "What else?"

"From what I heard from him and Georgette, along with my failures I believed that I was a disruptive child who was selfish and always up to no good."

With the missing pieces now found, Malinda was able to have a better picture of the puzzle. Her fear of the dark was from the sexual attack. She understood why she always slept with blankets over her head in fear that she might see a shape or a shadow of something lurking about in the room. Up until now, covering her eyes was the only way she could fool herself into believing that no harm would come to her and she could fall asleep. At times it was hot under the covers and breathing was difficult. As a grown woman she knew it was strange not to have grown out of that. Malinda remembered how difficult it was during the first attempted relaxation exercise to sit still and resist the urge to panic while being alone in a bedroom, even during daylight. Thanks to the recalled memory, the answer was identified to why she felt vulnerable to an unexpected attack in the safety of her bed.

Malinda also identified why she used to avoid crying when it was appropriate to grieve. She remembered how her daddy had prevented her from making any sound with his hand over her mouth and hearing him command her not to cry and not to scream. She understood why she restrained herself from screaming, even during difficult childbirth. She understood why she could not cry or grieve to express the loss of both her parents, a brother and sister-in-law at their quadruple funeral. It was as though the suppressed memory kept poking Malinda to get a response to the memory of that night when her daddy stood beside her bed just before he violated her.

I Told Him "No!"

A final memory from her childhood was very ambiguous until one day when a neighbor named Jim invited Malinda out for a ride on his four wheeler. She knew him for two years since she moved to the acreage. He was a mild mannered fellow that got along good with all the neighbors. They were friends that were attracted to each other. As they rode through the ditch and up into the forest, they came to his property line. Jim stopped to remove a small tree that had fallen on the fence. They continued to ride along the fence and stopped now and then to remove other small trees and branches that had fallen the same way. Malinda stepped down from the machine to help Jim when, out of nowhere, she suddenly became afraid of him, thinking that she was in great danger of being raped by him and no one would hear her screams. There was no signal of such an action from Jim. They got back on the four wheeler and the ride was bumpy. Jim took her through his acreage and came to a field filled with daisies and other wild flowers. Malinda marveled at the awesome sight. As they continued to ride, he looked after Malinda well, making sure she was sitting comfortably and securely so she wouldn't fall off the machine. After a half hour or so Jim drove Malinda home.

That evening Malinda pondered about her strange reaction while in the woods with Jim. She didn't want to ignore any red flags that would indicate that Jim might be dangerous. What was it about him that was so frightening? She asked herself. Then, something crossed her mind about when she was 8 years old. The four-wheeler ride reminded her of a particular day while watching her father mending the fence around the farm. Her father had his tractor hitched to a trailer full of fence posts. As he got on his tractor, Malinda asked if she could come along. Her father grunted, "Get on." Malinda sat on the back of the trailer with the fence posts. They drove off to a pasture. Malinda enjoyed the bumps when running over the many rocks along the way. She remembered how it was a bright sunny day. As they rode along, she saw many wildflowers. Her father came to a barb wire fence. They drove slowly along side of it and her father stopped to replace any damaged posts. Malinda watched her father pull out the old post and use a sledge hammer to pound in the new one. After a broken segment of the fence was fixed, they both resumed their riding positions and continued the inspection along the fence line. They got to the edge of the forest. The same routine reoccurred where her father would disembark his tractor and fix another post. Malinda stood beside him. She was wearing a cotton dress which the breeze made it wave in the wind. There were no conversations between the two which was normal for them.

The pleasant time with her father suddenly took an awful turn. Her father took her by the hand and forcibly pulled her into the woods. Malinda knew exactly what her father intended to do. She recognized the look on his face. Malinda drew back but she could not pull away from his hold. A cold and frightful demeanor came about him. He was unresponsive and acted like a robot. In an attempt to break his trance, Malinda yelled, "no daddy, no," she opposed. He forced Malinda down on the ground. Malinda screamed, "No, No!" Dried sticks from the forest floor dug into her back. She knew that he was going to hurt her in *that* way again. She hit him in the face and on his baldhead but it only made him more forceful. He got rough and he held her down by her forearms. She saw a close up of his coldness that had a fixed grip on him. She remembered it was like some kind of force overrode any moral convictions or sanity he might have left. Then he put his large hand over her mouth. She could smell the stench of cigarette tobacco on his smoke stained fingers. He removed her panties and penetrated her. She was unable to manage this amount of pain and she thought that she was going to die. Unable to leave, she departed mentally and passed out.

Unlike the first rape, this time Malinda did not confront her dad nor went to her mother for help. The pain in and around her vagina reminded her what just happened but Malinda suffered through it and remained silent. She blocked out the painful parts of this rape and only remembered the happy parts of that day. Incest took her virginity; her trust and her right to say, "No."

After this memory relapse, Malinda understood the origin of why she would freeze and be unable to say,"No," during unwanted sexual advances. She believed it was useless to say "no," and that it was a word that meant nothing. Malinda had always suffered from locked hips. Sitting with both legs crossed over each other in a yoga position was painful and something she could never do. She sought doctors, chiropractors and a physio-therapist about the ailment. Medical examinations ruled out arthritis and degenerative bone diseases. Both a doctor and a physio-therapist said it was a bone deformity and that she must have been born that way. Malinda remembered the strength she had to go through this on her own.

Malinda hired a man named Reverend Jeremy. He came highly recommended with a degree in psychology and accreditations in trauma recovery. One evening, he held a special gathering for healing at his church. Malinda went with a friend. He led those present into a prayer to ask God for healing. All of a sudden Malinda began to cry. The Reverend asked her why she was crying and Malinda answered with a shout, "No." I told him, No! But he wouldn't stop!" "Stop what?" the reverend asked Malinda. She sobbed and answered, "My daddy hurt me." The reverend understood what Malinda meant. With much compassion he said to her, "no child should ever have to experience trauma of the sort." Malinda held the temples of her head and thought it would help her remain sane during the memory. Strangely, her hip muscles and lower back hurt more than ever. Afterwards the bones of her hips would sometimes move differently like a shifting. The adjoined muscles also moved differently causing a clicking sound and more pain. The memory was back along with its physical after effect.

A few months later, on Easter weekend, Malinda went for a country ride with the Pastor Lloyd and his wife. On their way back home, they visited an elderly woman who was ill and housebound. While there, they all held hands and prayed for her and one another. Malinda asked for continued healing of her hips and muscles. After the prayer, Malinda said, "Both my hips just cracked!" Then the old woman said, "My neck cracked." She explained that for many years, a neck injury had caused her to have difficulty breathing. Malinda humorously said, "We both cracked at the same time!" Malinda's hip bones were back in place. Later at home, to test the healing, she sat on the floor and crossed her legs one over the other with ease and there was no pain whatsoever. This was another healing from a string of physical ailments caused by rape. She sat comfortably on the floor and thought about the first Easter when Christ died on the cross; He was heard saying, "*It is complete.*" Her thoughts then turned to understand that while facing incestuous memories that she would not have remained sane unless before the recalls had first forgiven her father for *everything* he did to her. Through the pain of remembering, forgiveness was already etched in her heart and she forgave also what would later be disclosed. Because of the miraculous forgiveness which took place before the recalls, Malinda could express normal anger during the return of her lost memories; but not forgiving never entered the picture.

Malinda reflected on the forgiveness that had allowed her to bring the scattered pieces of her memory and life back together to make them whole. She remembered the ants and how they worked hard to rebuild their mound. After all, the little ants had taught her well that to live in a forward direction meant there was no room for unforgiveness along the way!

Spirit Re-Connected

Even though the memories of incest can still cause her sadness, she is grateful for remembering. The missing memories had always made her feel like an incomplete woman, one that had missing parts. Going through the pain of facing the truth gave her a precious gift. With the memories intact she is now transformed into a whole and complete woman. She is able to be true to herself and seek to receive approval only from her Maker. Along with the memories, her true identity has emerged and is connected to her spirit. Malinda is now reconnected and complete. She has her memories and emotions, and is generally at peace with them.

Having found this treasure of oneness deep within her sacred space, she now identifies with Christ who helped her to stand. He was the prince in shining armor that loved her. She keeps Christ and the Holy Scriptures close to her heart. There she finds comfort in the passages that connect with her hard-earned truths. Her deep interest in the scriptures fascinates her, especially when the readings coincide directly with many of her visions, for example, Proverbs 5:19 in particular grasped her attention: *"A loving doe, a graceful deer - may her breasts satisfy you always, may you ever be captivated by her love."* These words described her most primal need of nurture and acceptance that she had discovered in one of her first visualization exercises. Proverbs 30:25, a verse dedicated to the ants, reminded her of how, as a young child, she had marvelled at the little creatures: *"how they are so little yet massive gatherers of food for winter."* This was much more than mere coincidence. Malinda is convinced that early in childhood her spirit, which guided her and showed her life lessons, was indeed the Spirit that was connected to God, which she now refers to as the Holy Spirit. This was later confirmed in Romans 8 where she joyfully read: *"The Spirit Himself bears witness with our spirit that we are children of God."*

Malinda's many years of work, peer counseling and education resulted in her reconnection with her ultimate Father God. Her healing process was complete. However, she still finds it difficult at times to relate with the opposite sex, but she is able to bring a quick end to a wrong relationship. She has learned to live alone happily. Her feelings do not always coincide with her newly found knowledge but she is kind to herself and gives her feelings time to adapt to willingness for growth. The feelings that used to be in charge of her actions are stubborn and do not readily want to let go of control but healing defeats that. Her new behaviors need practice until they are fully learned. The experience is similar to a child learning how to walk for the first time. The toddler watches others walk and knows about walking but has not yet learned how to do it. With the will to walk, the child becomes willing to try and fall. Holding onto something or to someone's hand, the child learns the first steps. Then, with a lot of attempts, the child finally walks. Malinda knows that her healthier choices will one day occur as naturally as walking. With practice, the process develops and comes to full maturity.

Malinda continues to teach that to be consciously alive means to celebrate one's successes and to have the ability to recognize mistakes when they happen. She recognizes the red flags of her old behaviors and switches her thoughts to appropriately process her feelings. She forgives others and herself and continues to move forward. She believes that victory is achieved from within. It takes courage to seek healing. Fear of what might be unveiled had kept Malinda in a black tunnel, which veered her away from a hopeful future. Divine Guidance gave her the strength to continue walking toward the light each step of the way on the road to truth and love. She learned that love is found within and that kind of love, no one can withhold from her ever again. Like a homing device, her spirit constantly sought to be connected with love.

Malinda discovered that while she had worked hard to erase the traumatic events of her childhood, joyful memories also got hidden in the amnesia. Trauma was blotted out, but so were most of the memories from the years of incest. Like Steeve at the counseling centre, Malinda discovered that the switch that turns off an emotion turns them all off, not just one of them. In Malinda's case, this certainly proved to be true. With the return of painful memories Malinda found delight in remembering also the pleasant moments of her childhood. Little things that may seem insignificant to someone else meant that happiness also was present in her childhood. For example, she remembered the smell of that new leather schoolbag which her mother bought at the start of her third year in school. A present to comfort Malinda because she had to repeat that year. Malinda got a new bag instead of one passed down from her siblings. There was the smell of a new doll, which her mother bought for her birthday. The doll had blond hair and blue eyes, she remembers, just like Malinda's and it was not just any ordinary doll! This one had rooted hair that could be combed and her body could be submerged in water for a bath. Any smell like that of the new doll can bring back the memory of many happy hours of play.

Remembering positive things from her childhood, one most precious memory was of Christmas one year when her mother gave a card to her. Malinda sometimes takes it out and remembers how, when she was twelve years of age and returning home from midnight mass, her mother had composed a poem in the Christmas card. Her mother wrote,

> *"I received gifts wrapped in papers of different colors but*
> *the nicest one*
> *of all was one*
> *I can't eat or touch or see,*
> *Yet worth more than gold to me.*
> *It's the carols that you sang*
> *In the church while Christmas rang.*
> *Merry Christmas."*

At the time, Malinda placed little value on her mother's Christmas card but today, as a healed individual, she cherishes the card and reads it each Christmas. Once a year she reflects on the times she would be dejected about having to give up so many lunch hours at school for choir practice. She now realizes that the time spent had not robbed her of anything, but had actually strengthened her gift of singing. When reading her mother's Christmas card, Malinda realizes how much the singing had touched her mother's heart. That makes all the missed recesses worth giving up. Malinda gave her mother a gift that could not be store-bought. In return, she received something precious also: her mother's gift of poetry expressing heartfelt gratitude that still lasts long after her death.

Wholeness was not obtained as the result of conventional methods, counseling and education. These alone would have brought Malinda about halfway to her destination. She knows she could not arrive without assistance from her Knight in shining armor. Today, Christ remains her closest confidant and healer. More than ever, she stands on her belief that he came to earth to show mankind the way to the Father who is love.

While sleeping one night Malinda had a dream. She saw her daddy's face morbid from death. He was lying in a grey coffin. In the dream, Malinda said to him, "I always loved you." Then she kissed her dead father on the forehead and said "Goodbye." The coffin became completely empty. Suddenly standing beside Malinda appeared Christ. He said, "He is gone." Malinda asked, "Why, after all these years, is today the day that I bid my father a last goodbye?" In unspoken words, Christ reminded her that it was Father's Day. In a spiritual fashion an understanding came to Malinda that all negative effects from her earthly father had been released. Within that moment, the negative grip these effects held on her left forever. After the dream, Malinda felt freedom from all obsessive thoughts about hurt and disappointments that originated from her father. Wailings of never getting her father's approval were no longer part of Malinda's emotional state. She could move on with her life without carrying that heavy lie that told her she did not qualify for love.

Freed from her past, Malinda can now experience her present life while looking forward to the future. She keeps her special relationship with Christ and maintains a daily routine of thankfulness and love. Each morning she asks for Divine Guidance to steer her every step. Each evening she concludes her prayer by listing the many blessings of her day. She sleeps peacefully without covering her head with blankets knowing that her only source of love is God. As a result, any newly acquired resentments and animosities fade away quickly. Every morning is welcomed. Malinda started her healing journey from within, from Serenity and back to love.

Life Returns the Favor

In a particularly meaningful devotional called "Life Returns the Favor" from the website called The Daily Motivator, Malinda read as it accurately described a reflection of the many adversities she had to overcome during her healing journey. (Permission obtained from Ralph Marston, owner of The Daily Motivator website.)

Life Returns the Favor
By Ralph Marston

When you encounter resistance, it means you are moving forward. When you come across a challenge, it means you have reached the point where you can successfully meet that challenge. Life becomes more rewarding as it becomes more demanding. You are destined to achieve, and each successive achievement positions you for an even greater, more challenging achievement.

Each new challenge is an opportunity to stretch beyond your previous limits. Most of the advantages you enjoy today were born in the difficulties through which you traveled in days past.

Every day brings a new way for you to more fully give of yourself. It is by so giving, in ways that are familiar and in ways not yet imagined, that you create the life you most sincerely desire.

In everything there is treasure to be found. The richest treasures are those that ask the most of you, for they resonate wholly with your deepest purpose.

Delight in the living beauty of each challenging effort. Give your best to life and life returns the favor, a million times over.

Permission to use other material
----- Original Message -----
From: "Ralph Marston - The Daily Motivator"
<ralph@dailymotivator.com>
To: <ifm@mts.net>
Sent: Thursday, January 31, 2008 8:33 AM
Subject: Daily Motivator Reprint Permission

> ➤ Your Reprint Permission Request Has Been Approved
> >
> > You have permission to reprint The Daily Motivator
> > message from January 31, 2008 titled "Life returns the
> > favor" in your book as you have described below.
> >
> > In place of the original copyright notice, please substitute
> > the following two lines:
> >
> > Copyright 2008 Ralph S. Marston, Jr. Used by permission.
> > Originally published in "The Daily Motivator" at
>   www.dailymotivator.com
> >
> >
> > Permission is given only for a one-time, non-exclusive
> > reprint of the one message described above and does not
> > include permission for use of any other material from
> > The Daily Motivator website or e-mail edition.
> >
> > Sincerely,
> > Ralph S. Marston, Jr.
> > Author & Publisher - The Daily Motivator
> >
> > Details of Permission request:
> >
> > Your name - Isabelle Fiola
> > Company - ISABELLE FIOLA MINISTRIES/ IFM LIFE
>   SKILLS CHURCH/ IFM SERENITY HOUSE
> > Phone - ifm@mts.net
> > E-mail - ifm@mts.net
> > Name of publication - in the process of writing book

> Type of publication - book
> Approx. number of copies - thousands
> Approx. publication date - uncertain
>
>
➢
➢

ISABELLE A. FIOLA WANTS TO
HEAR FROM YOU!!!

Tell Isabelle how My Daddy Hurt Me has impacted your life in a positive way.

Send a letter through the mail:

Book Testimonial

Y Fiola

30 Georges Forest Pl.

Winnipeg, Mb (Canada)

R2H 3H5

OR

Email Isabelle at iafiola@ymail.com

Please note: Testimonials received will become the property of the author, Isabelle A. Fiola and may be printed or used for book evaluation and reviews.